SHARED FOUNDATIONS

Curate

SHARED FOUNDATIONS SERIES

I. **INQUIRE,** by Lori E. Donovan

II. **INCLUDE,** by Julie Stivers

III. **COLLABORATE,** by Mary Catherine Coleman

IV. **CURATE,** by Daniella LaShaun Smith and Len Bryan

V. **EXPLORE,** by Sarah Culp Searles

VI. **ENGAGE,** by Kathryn Roots Lewis and Marcia A. Mardis

SHARED FOUNDATIONS

Curate

DANIELLA LASHAUN SMITH AND LEN BRYAN

ALA Editions
CHICAGO | 2024

AASL American Association of School Librarians
TRANSFORMING LEARNING

ISBN: 978-0-8389-1918-7 (paper)

Library of Congress Cataloging-in-Publication Data

Names: Smith, Daniella, author. | Bryan, Len, author.
Title: Curate / Daniella LaShaun Smith and Len Bryan.
Description: Chicago : ALA Editions, AASL, 2024. | Series: Shared foundations series ; IV | Includes bibliographical references and index. | Summary: "Curate helps connect learners to resources in more thoughtful, meaningful ways. This practical guide features an examination of school library policy placing Curate in context; field notes from practicing school librarians implementing the Curate Shared Foundation; learning trajectories in grade-level bands, offering examples of Curate in action and ways to scaffold learning; a sample alignment of Curate Competencies in the AASL Standards Framework for Learners with the Common Core State Standards; lesson starters, case studies, and best practices that demonstrate inspiring and effective strategies; and questions to promote engagement with reflective practice"—Provided by publisher.
Identifiers: LCCN 2023029976 | ISBN 9780838919187 (paperback)
Subjects: LCSH: School libraries—Aims and objectives—United States. | School libraries—Collection development—United States. | School libraries—Information technology—United States. | School librarian participation in curriculum planning—United States. | Libraries and schools—United States.
Classification: LCC Z675.S3 S65195 2023 | DDC 025.2/1878—dc23/eng/20230801
LC record available at https://lccn.loc.gov/2023029976

♾ This paper meets the requirements of ANSI/NISO Z39.48-1992 (Permanence of Paper).

Printed in the United States of America
28 27 26 25 24   5 4 3 2 1

Purchases of AASL publications and products fund advocacy, leadership, professional development, and standards initiatives for school librarians nationally.

ALA Editions purchases fund advocacy, awareness, and accreditation programs for library professionals worldwide.

SHARED FOUNDATION IV

Curate

KEY COMMITMENT

Make meaning for oneself and others by collecting, organizing, and sharing resources of personal relevance.

Contents

Acknowledgments

From Daniella . . . I want to thank my husband, Herbert L. Smith Jr., because he is my champion and confidant. I applaud my University of North Texas doctoral students—Diana Colby, Diane Gill, Ijay Kaz-Onyeakazi, and Stacie Milburn—for being so gracious with their time and input. Stephanie Book, Jamie Santoro, and Sylvia Norton are the best for trusting me to work on this project. I feel blessed to have such wonderful people in my life.

From Len . . . I would first like to thank my wife, Alison Granzin Bryan, for all her support, both as I worked on *Curate* and as I have moved through my career and professional life. Her patience, understanding, and flexibility are unmatched. I'd also like to thank the school librarians I have had the pleasure of working with in Texas, Oregon, and Colorado, as well as around the world, who continue to put their learners first, often in spite of incredible obstacles. I see you, and I applaud you and your work.

Series Introduction

The Shared Foundations series from the American Association of School Librarians (AASL) examines the six Shared Foundations that anchor the comprehensive approach to teaching and learning in the *National School Library Standards for Learners, School Librarians, and School Libraries.* The Shared Foundations—Inquire, Include, Collaborate, Curate, Explore, and Engage—represent the core concepts that all learners, school librarians, and school libraries develop and promote in their K–12 learning environment.

Each of the six books in this series is dedicated to the deep exploration of a single Shared Foundation. Although each of the Shared Foundations supports its own inherent priorities, it cannot be implemented in isolation. The writing process used by the authors created a series of books that, like the AASL Standards Frameworks, are unique and yet parallel each other. Common elements are found throughout the series:

- A balance between theoretical discussion, practical strategies, and implementation examples, promoting reflection and creativity
- Development of the Competencies and Alignments for the Learner, School Librarian, and School Library in all four Domains—Think, Create, Share, and Grow
- Differences in application and assessment across grades K–12, promoting a growth mindset and envisioning outcomes for all learners, whether student learners, school librarians, or other educators
- An emphasis on personalized learning experiences, project-based learning, and authenticity of learning and projects
- Challenges addressed, illustrating ways to implement the Shared Foundations in various environments and levels of support

Questions for the Reflective Practitioner conclude each chapter, allowing readers to consider the application of concepts specific to their own learning communities and stimulate nuanced professional conversations. For ease of reference, readers also will find the AASL Standards Integrated Framework for the relevant Shared Foundation included in this work.

AASL and its series authors hope that this immersive and dedicated examination of the Shared Foundations will help school library professionals deepen their understandings, broaden their perspectives, make connections for personal relevance, and innovate and reflect on their practice with a professional community.

For more information about the *National School Library Standards*, and to access the latest implementation assistance resources, visit standards.aasl.org.

SHARED FOUNDATION IV.

Curate

Domain	LEARNER DOMAINS AND COMPETENCIES	SCHOOL LIBRARIAN DOMAINS AND COMPETENCIES
A. Think	**Learners act on an information need by:** 1. Determining the need to gather information. 2. Identifying possible sources of information. 3. Making critical choices about information sources to use.	**School librarians challenge learners to act on an information need by:** 1. Modeling the response to a need to gather and organize information. 2. Designing opportunities for learners to explore possible information sources. 3. Guiding learners to make critical choices about information sources to use.
B. Create	**Learners gather information appropriate to the task by:** 1. Seeking a variety of sources. 2. Collecting information representing diverse perspectives. 3. Systematically questioning and assessing the validity and accuracy of information. 4. Organizing information by priority, topic, or other systematic scheme.	**School librarians promote information gathering appropriate to the task by:** 1. Sharing a variety of sources. 2. Encouraging the use of information representing diverse perspectives. 3. Fostering the questioning and assessing of validity and accuracy of information. 4. Providing tools and strategies to organize information by priority, topic, or other systematic scheme.
C. Share	**Learners exchange information resources within and beyond their learning community by:** 1. Accessing and evaluating collaboratively constructed information sites. 2. Contributing to collaboratively constructed information sites by ethically using and reproducing others' work. 3. Joining with others to compare and contrast information derived from collaboratively constructed information sites.	**School librarians contribute to and guide information resource exchange within and beyond the school learning community by:** 1. Facilitating opportunities to access and evaluate collaboratively constructed information sites. 2. Devising pathways for learners to contribute to collaboratively constructed information sites by ethically using and reproducing others' work. 3. Directing learners to join others to compare and contrast information derived from collaboratively constructed information sites.
D. Grow	**Learners select and organize information for a variety of audiences by:** 1. Performing ongoing analysis of and reflection on the quality, usefulness, and accuracy of curated resources. 2. Integrating and depicting in a conceptual knowledge network their understanding gained from resources. 3. Openly communicating curation processes for others to use, interpret, and validate.	**School librarians show learners how to select and organize information for a variety of audiences by:** 1. Engaging learners in ongoing analysis of and reflection on the quality, usefulness, and accuracy of curated resources. 2. Formulating tasks that help learners to integrate and depict in a conceptual knowledge network learners' understanding gained from resources. 3. Making opportunities for learners to openly communicate curation processes for others to use, interpret, and validate.

KEY COMMITMENT

Make meaning for oneself and others by collecting, organizing, and sharing resources of personal relevance.

SCHOOL LIBRARY DOMAINS AND ALIGNMENTS — **The school library facilitates the Key Commitment to and Competencies of CURATE**	Domain
The school library provides problem-based learning experiences and environments by: 1. Using resources and technology to foster inquiry and scaffold mastery of skills necessary for learning to progress. 2. Adopting a dynamic collection-development plan to ensure that adequate resources reflect current and in-depth knowledge. 3. Focusing on the effective use of a wide range of resources to foster information skills appropriate to content areas.	**A. Think**
The school library promotes selection of appropriate resources and tools for information use by: 1. Demonstrating and documenting how resources and technology are used to address information needs. 2. Providing opportunities for all members of the school community to develop information and technology skills needed to promote the transfer of information-related problem-solving strategies across all disciplines. 3. Employing a dynamic collection policy that includes selection and retention criteria for all materials within the collection. 4. Implementing an administratively approved and endorsed policy that clearly addresses procedures for handling material challenges. 5. Designing and providing adequate, appropriate space for library resources, services, and activities.	**B. Create**
The school library facilitates the contribution and exchange of information within and among learning communities by: 1. Providing an environment in which resources that support the school's curriculum and learning goals can be collaboratively selected and developed. 2. Including and tracking collection materials in a system that uses standardized approaches to description and location. 3. Establishing policies that promote effective acquisition, description, circulation, sharing, and access to resources within and beyond the school day. 4. Maintaining procedures that ensure user confidentiality and promote unimpeded access to materials by staff members and learners.	**C. Share**
The school library engages the learning community in exploring resources by: 1. Describing, organizing, and promoting the collection for maximum and effective uses for multiple learning applications. 2. Maintaining a collection of sufficient breadth and currency to be pertinent to the school's program of studies. 3. Supporting access through a schedule that allows use by learners and staff at time of need. 4. Using local and external data to inform ongoing adjustments to the scope of the resource collection, and its audiences, formats, and applications.	**D. Grow**

Preface

I hope you don't mind my telling you why the Curate Shared Foundation is so important. The entire country has been through so much during the past three years. We have had to find our way through a crisis that we were not prepared for. As school librarians, we used our ability to *Inquire, Include, Collaborate, Curate,* and *Explore* to *Engage* our school communities. Although we felt unprepared, we still had the foundational skills that enabled us to shine through the darkness like lighthouses.

We faced an enormous challenge. Yet we have grown—within our global community, in our country, in our local locations, and as a profession. Evolution is indeed essential for society. It is with evolution in mind that I write my part of the preface. The Curate Shared Foundation is my favorite Shared Foundation because it induces the evolutionary process.

As you read the book and examine our discussion of the Curate Shared Foundation, you will see that we (school librarians) are asking learners to evolve, and to do that within our foundational competencies, we are charged with accepting the need to change, to move ourselves and our school communities toward questioning what we know so we can find new information. Without the curation and questioning of knowledge, we cease to learn. As Nobel Peace Prize winner Kofi Annan (1997) said, "Knowledge is power. Information is liberating. Education is the premise of progress, in every society, in every family."

We have always emphasized learning and education in my family. My parents grew up in the rural Deep South where Jim Crow laws were prevalent. As youth, they thirsted for knowledge when access to education and books was discouraged. Years before I earned my degrees, my parents described to me what I came to know as information poverty. Information poverty is a deadly disease that continues to be prevalent. It is sinister when the quality of life suffers because of a lack of access to correct information.

When I became an educator and librarian, my parents expressed pride because I had access to something they had dreamed of when they were children. I had a special job . . . and a calling to fulfill. So when I was invited to write about the Curate Shared Foundation, I was delighted. It is a privilege to coauthor a book designed to assist learners and educators with curating knowledge and embracing intellectual freedom. May we never forget the power of school librarianship.

—Daniella LaShaun Smith

As I reflect on the very long process of working on this book, I keep thinking about resilience. When I began drafting *Curate* in 2018, I had just started working in Denver Public Schools. It is now near the end of 2022, and we have survived a global pandemic, political and social turmoil, and increasingly bizarre challenges—not only to library books but also to our jobs, our safety, and the education profession in general. We have lost colleagues, friends, and loved ones, and our world and work look very different.

School librarians have faced unprecedented obstacles as what were once relatively rare and usually civil conversations about instructional materials and library books have devolved into polarizing, politically motivated assaults on our character and intentions. Our curation policies and practices, a core component of our work, have been called into question and publicly ridiculed for political gain. Many have chosen to retire or leave the profession as these attacks persisted. I personally reconsidered my career choice several times within those four years and seriously pondered the possibility of leaving education.

And still we persist, working within our schools to ensure that our learners have unimpeded access to information, no matter how uncomfortable that access might be to some who would rather shelter learners than trust them to curate information for themselves. We continue to curate information in all its forms, to instruct our learners in the power of information and ideas, and to advocate that how we curate information matters. We work with educators and learners to provide tools and training to help them *think* for themselves, *create* learning products that demonstrate their knowledge in innovative ways, *share* that knowledge both within the school and around the world, and *grow* as learners, curators, and global citizens.

I have been fortunate to serve as a librarian and school library administrator in three U.S. states, five school districts, and one state agency. In all these places and in all my experiences, the Curate Shared Foundation consistently comes up as a central component of my work. As a result of working on this book, my understanding of curation in school libraries now extends far beyond library collection development, though that is still a fundamental part of our work. The Curate Shared Foundation is inextricably tied to instruction and is interwoven throughout all the Shared Foundations in our *National School Library Standards*.

My hopes are that the ideas and examples in this book will contribute something of value to our profession and that you, the reader, also practice curation as you move through the chapters—making meaning for yourself and others as you absorb and reflect on the text, tables, illustrations, and examples from your school library peers.

School librarianship continues to evolve, with new tools, techniques, ideas, and yes, even challenges. As we look to the future, our Shared Foundations and Common Beliefs provide a solid foundation of library science fundamentals on which we can build innovative, responsive, and student-focused resources, instruction, and programming. In an age when our learners face increasing challenges to their freedom to access and use information, school librarians are perfectly positioned to practice, teach, and model the Curate Shared Foundation, which is essential to learning.

—Len Bryan

Introduction: What Drives Our Work?

The Curate Shared Foundation is defined in the *National School Library* *Standards for Learners, School Librarians, and School Libraries* as "[making] meaning for oneself and others by collecting, organizing, and sharing resources of personal relevance" (American Association of School Librarians [AASL] 2018, 94). The purpose of this book is to help you, no matter where you are in your school library career, whether you are a school librarian, school library supervisor, school library professor, or a pre-service school librarian, to understand and apply curation as illustrated in the *National School Library Standards* to your practice, your ongoing professional learning, and your instruction and collaboration with learners and other educators. If you are a school administrator, our hope is for you to understand more deeply what the school librarian profession calls us to do and inspire your school librarian with high expectations when it comes to curating for your school community. Supporting your school librarian in their curation activities can positively impact academic achievement in your school. In addition, research supports the benefits of having highly qualified school librarians (Scholastic 2016).

Curation is a needed activity throughout the academic years so that learners can then effectively curate for themselves, no matter what they choose to pursue after graduation (Kist 2022). Connecting the human activity of curation across time and disciplines outside school librarianship provides a compelling case for curation services in our schools. Moreover, the connection to our behaviors also supports school librarians as they teach curation skills and provide opportunities for learners to practice curation.

Common Beliefs

One of the most compelling features of the *National School Library Standards* is the set of Common Beliefs (AASL 2018, 11–14). These six statements do a terrific job of capturing and expressing the core pillars of school librarianship. The Common Beliefs consider our experiences in a complicated, messy, and ever-changing profession and condense them into a few key statements that are helpful and instructive in various scenarios. The Common Beliefs, as articulated on the AASL Standards web portal (AASL, n.d.-b), provide both a firm foundation for the work of librarians and a clear sense of the direction school districts should take as they strive to continuously improve school libraries. We have added commentary to each of the Common Beliefs to connect them to the Curate Shared Foundation and to the focus of the chapters to follow.

Common Beliefs

1. The school library is a unique and essential part of a learning community.
2. Qualified school librarians lead effective school libraries.
3. Learners should be prepared for college, career, and life.
4. Reading is the core of personal and academic competency.
5. Intellectual freedom is every learner's right.
6. Information technologies must be appropriately integrated and equitably available.

Source: AASL 2018, 11.

1. The school library is a unique and essential part of a learning community.

Building and strengthening connections are core functions of the work of school librarians. We connect learners, other educators, administrators, and our communities to information, to the world outside our school walls, and to each other. School librarians create strong connections between our communities and the love of reading. We teach our colleagues, learners, and the community how to access, evaluate, and use both traditional and emerging sources of information ethically and productively. Our instruction empowers our school communities to contribute to the advancement of our society.

School librarians are unique educators for many reasons, chief among which is our provision of resources curated for our schools. While collecting and facilitating access to a wide variety of learning resources, school librarians create connections between academic knowledge and a deep understanding of our world. Curation has always been a core part of librarianship. Chapter 1 briefly explores the history of school libraries and librarians and how they have curated materials through the ages.

2. Qualified school librarians lead effective school libraries.

Change is a constant, and we must not only embrace it and what it means for our communities but also create opportunities to lead change for our organizations. Gone are the days when school librarians presided over stacks of well-organized books in a dull, authoritarian, adult-focused environment (Gross 2022). Significant time is now spent outside the physical library, *engaging* with our community, *exploring* the world of virtual works online, *curating* resources in easily accessible spaces, *collaborating* with our colleagues, building *inclusive* library spaces, both physical and virtual, and leading our school community in deep *inquiry* that goes far beyond the mere collection of bits of knowledge. It is truly the most exciting time to be a school librarian!

Adequate staffing and resources vary according to settings. As a result, AASL emphasizes that every child, regardless of the type or size of school they attend, deserves access to a full-time, certified school librarian, with dedicated support staff and budget. These factors are essential for transforming teaching and learning (AASL 2019b). Advocacy is discussed in chapters 6 and 7.

3. Learners should be prepared for college, career, and life.

How we address the Curate Shared Foundation plays a tremendous role in how we contribute to the mission of our districts and schools. School librarians help every learner achieve academic success and curate resources that learners need. Effective library programming supports equity by ensuring that accessible materials serve as mirrors, windows, and sliding glass doors (Bishop 1990) for all learners.

Teaching learners, stakeholders, and colleagues to curate diverse resources is important in an information society. We provide access and opportunities for learners to connect with college, careers, and their lives after school through curated resources. The role of curation in instruction is discussed in chapters 3, 4, and 5.

4. Reading is the core of personal and academic competency.

Even with the proliferation of learning opportunities through digital audio and video, the visual-cognitive discipline of reading print is still our society's dominant means of developing reading comprehension skills (Sparks 2021). School librarians curate high-quality information for our schools in a wide variety of formats—print and digital resources, video, audio, augmented and virtual reality—all have a place in school library collections. We present all these to our communities within a culture of reading, engaging our communities through the power of story and encouraging them to pursue lifelong learning for its own sake. Aspects of nontraditional curation are discussed in chapters 6, 8, and 9.

5. Intellectual freedom is every learner's right.

Intellectual freedom is embedded within the core values of librarianship (American Library Association Council 2019). School librarians facilitate intellectual freedom by facilitating access to diverse viewpoints, intellectual tools, and spaces to read, view, and listen to discourse. Curation efforts must be inclusive of different perspectives, free from censorship, and supported by strong collection-development policies, and we must actively lead our communities in modeling respect for the viewpoints of those whose experiences differ from our own. Intellectual freedom as an essential component of collection-development and general school library policies is explored in chapter 2.

6. Information technologies must be appropriately integrated and equitably available.

Curating technologies and teaching learners to use them effectively are the responsibility of every educator (ISTE 2023). School librarians must be leaders in these efforts by ensuring that technology and connectivity are enhanced with resources that increase multiple literacy skills. Technology is a powerful tool for engaging our communities, creating transformational works, and finding opportunities to enhance the quality of our lives. Leveraging technology for curation is explored in chapter 7.

The Content of This Book

We have divided this book into four sections. *Part I: Placing Curate in Context* discusses the history of curation and how it has evolved. You will learn how other professions curate and about the policies that school librarians use to guide curation behaviors. *Part II: Curation for Learners* considers how the entire school community comprises learners, regardless of their ages. You will learn how school librarians are teachers of curation who facilitate lifelong curation skills. *Part III: Beyond Books* explains how curation is more than just the traditional concept of collecting books. It involves an interactive process that draws from the knowledge of the entire school community. Finally, *Part IV: Curate in Practice* shares case studies from school librarians who understand curation best practices. You will also notice Field Notes placed throughout the book. These alerts include tips and reflections from school librarians about their curation practices.

We hope that upon completing this book, you will embrace and promote the Curate Shared Foundation as a guide for exceeding traditional school library collection development. The Curate Shared Foundation offers opportunities to expand how our profession situates collections within services to school communities. We hope you will feel empowered to use this information to improve student learning outcomes and the culture of your school community. Dynamic curation practices will assist you with reinforcing connections to your school, allowing you to prepare learners for lifelong learning and the transition to college and strengthening the school library as a hub for intellectual freedom and scholarly communication and as a provider of relevant, engaging materials.

PART I

Placing Curate in Context

1

Exploring Curation in Society

It's human nature to curate and surround ourselves with valuable things. Our ancestors have practiced curation for millennia—locating, evaluating, and organizing useful items to enhance their lives. Pointy sticks, sharp rocks, tasty plants, animal meat, and hides eventually found their way into these prehistoric collections. As they evolved, ancient humans learned through trial and error, experimentation, direct instruction, and imitation. They curated the finest resources to allow generations to thrive. These early forms of curation helped our hunter-gatherer ancestors ensure that the most intelligent humans survived to pass along their knowledge (Castro and Toro 2004).

Expanding Curation Beyond Survival

As survival became easier through technological innovations, our ancestors continued to curate, moving from pointy sticks to more advanced tools, art, religious objects, and, later, written works on tablets, parchment, scrolls, papyrus, codices, and eventually books. Of course, these written works and other tangible forms of human knowledge serve as the foundation of librarianship. Our profession has long revolved around collecting, storing, protecting, and circulating knowledge captured in writing. More recently, librarians' professional activities have expanded to include creating and providing access to services, such as instruction, programming, reference, and readers' advisory.

Collecting Is Not Curating

School librarianship is a relatively modern idea, unlike other types of librarianship. On the contrary, school libraries are primarily curated to support the school's curriculum. They offer opportunities for self-directed reading and serve the personal development needs of learners, educators, and their communities. For this reason, modern, learner-focused school libraries should not measure their curation success by the number of volumes but by their *usefulness*. Bigger is frequently not better, especially with school libraries. It is more beneficial to have a small, focused collection that serves the school's needs than to have an extensive, outdated collection that no one uses.

The term *curation* is often associated with the collection of "things" (Balzer 2015). Conversely, professionals who curate, as opposed to collectors, deliberately choose materials to meet specific needs. For instance, school libraries add materials to collections because they meet the school community's needs by supporting the curriculum. *Collecting* a pretty lamp is distinguished from *curating* a library collection by considering that curation focuses on others' needs to a great extent. Remember, we *collect* items for ourselves, and we *curate* items for others.

FIELD NOTE **Knowing Your Community**

Curation is more than just getting the right books for your school library. It's knowing the collection, the curriculum, the other educators, and your learners. It means anticipating the needs of the patrons and checking sources for the best possible fit for your library. Materials for all ages, abilities, cultures, and lifestyles are needed so each learner can feel seen.

—Trina Samson (elementary school librarian, Washington)

Curation as Practiced by Other Professions

School librarians are not the only professionals who curate as a central part of their work. We have just cultivated the practice through decades of holding professional conversations, developing and refining policies and procedures, and codifying practices. Our professional associations and formal education have facilitated the process.

Now that we have defined how curation relates to school librarianship, let's explore how it coincides with other professions that our learners may pursue. Although other professions may not define their work as curation, the practice and concept apply to several occupations and disciplines. For example, when we think of the word *curate*, our minds retrieve images of museum curators who collect items related to a specific period, theme, or artistic style. Museum curation is the most understood type of curation. However, curation facilitates the advancement of many professions. Fundamentally, curation is a foundational skill regardless of a learner's career path or personal interest.

TABLE 1.1 / **Curation by other professionals**

Profession	What They Curate	How They Curate	Why They Curate	How School Librarians Can Share Knowledge and Teach Skills to Prepare Learners for Curation
Journalist	Contacts	Through establishing relationships built on professional trust	To get inside information not readily available via press releases or news conferences	Focus on credibility, ethics, and interpersonal skills
Academic	Knowledge, journals	Through extensive reading, testing, and studying	To become experts in their fields and to publish and discover new theories and models of practice	Focus on exposing learners to an array of fields to pique interest
Contractor	Specialized tools, materials, and techniques	Through experience and learning from others	To become successful in their business and to gain clients	Focus on learning from experiences, growth mindset
Real estate agent	Knowledge	Through reading, study, and experience	To become successful in their business and to gain clients	Focus on interpersonal skills, the importance of research
Educator	Knowledge, tools	Through practice and professional development	To become more adept at teaching their learners and at sharing their knowledge with other educators	Focus on interpersonal skills and instilling a love of learning, as well as fostering cooperative opportunities

Table 1.1 features selected careers and how practitioners integrate curation into their professions. This list is not exhaustive. The purpose is to show how school librarians can make connections for learners using the Curate Shared Foundation as learners prepare for college, career, and life. The table also shows that curation takes place in many formats, such as people, facts, theories, methods, and skills. Consider the importance of the "items" curated by the professionals in table 1.1:

- Journalists: Without the contacts carefully curated by journalists, especially in investigative reporting, it would be difficult for society to maintain the

Fourth Estate (Tran 2016) and its vital checks on government and corporate power.

- Academics and scientists: The theories, hypotheses, and knowledge frameworks carefully curated by researchers and academics inform emerging practices and advances in their fields.
- General contractors: General contractors pass their knowledge of construction to apprentices and other building contractors to grow their businesses and build the infrastructure that enhances society.
- Real estate agents: Real estate agents collect, assess, and organize extensive knowledge bases to supplement their ongoing professional development. Their knowledge makes them valuable allies when buying or selling a property.
- Educators: Educators share curated knowledge through committee work, leadership roles, and professional learning networks so learners can benefit from the continuous evaluation of pedagogy.

It would be an excellent exercise to ask learners how curation skills might apply to their chosen careers. In addition, ask them why curation is essential in the profession and how their curation skills can affect society. This activity could be beneficial in the relatively common What Do You Want to Be When You Grow Up? projects in elementary schools, career exploration units, or assignments in secondary school.

As you complete the What Do You Want to Be When You Grow Up? exercise, notice in table 1.1 that each profession has an element of curated relationships. The association with peers is an important aspect of curation to discuss with learners.

Regarding professional practice as a school librarian, curation closely parallels social learning and how our learners curate peers. Forming childhood friendships is like developing friendships and professional contacts as adults. We locate, assess, and evaluate potential relationships in each case to determine their benefits.

Learning to develop professional learning networks (PLNs) to contribute to society makes learners influential members of the global community. Hence, curating relationships is a necessary part of building social capital. Carefully applying curation strategies to making friends and professional acquaintances, though mechanical, is an excellent way to select people with whom we can associate.

Similar to Other Professions, Yet So Different

After years of working in a field, extensive study, and a conscious effort to hone their craft, professionals become experts in their subject. Part of that expertise is a thorough knowledge of the resources they need to complete a task. School librarianship is simultaneously similar to and different from other professions that practice curation. School librarians must not only become experts at curating and using the tools but also become adept at knowing the needs of learners. School librarians show that we understand community needs enough to curate, recommend, and provide instruction on the right resource at the right time for the proper purpose. When we do our jobs well, we become the Swiss Army knife of education (figure 1.1), capable of performing various essential professional functions. Exemplar school librarians can employ an array of tools and thoughtfully access an intentionally curated knowledge base for their own use and the use of their school communities.

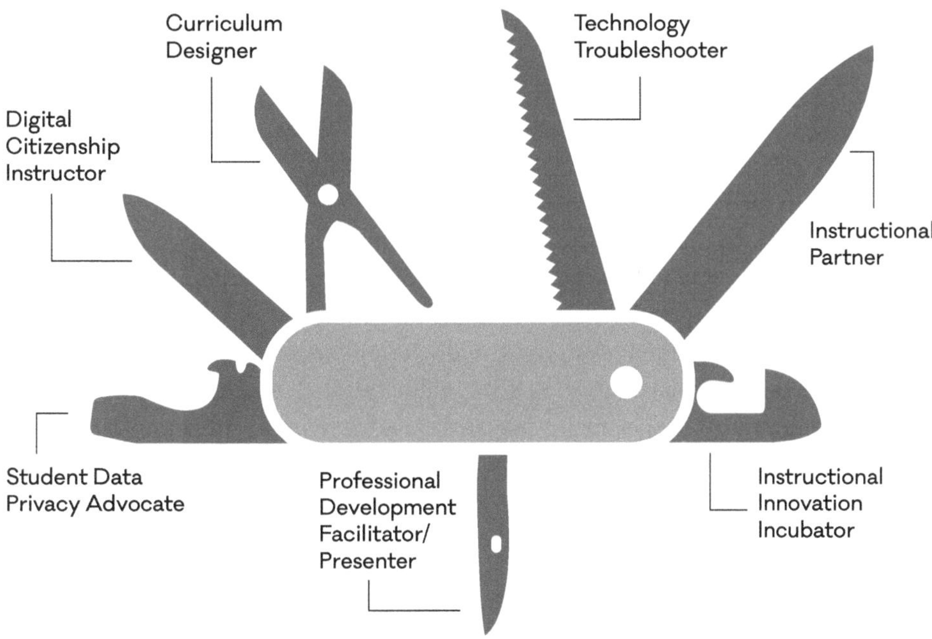

FIGURE 1.1 /
School librarians: Your school's Swiss Army knife

Considerations for Supporting Learning with Curation

One method of developing our knowledge base is to ask learners about their needs. Note that the term *learners* includes everyone in the school community, including the school librarian. Have conversations about current projects and the information or resources needed to enrich the learning process and to make it interesting. Endeavor to collaboratively develop learning products, curate resources, and display evidence of learning in the school library.

Engaging in conversations about assignments and school projects will provide opportunities to curate resources for learners. Reaching out to classroom educators and interacting during lunchtime will provide rich opportunities for making meaningful connections. These connections will help you become a Swiss Army knife of education who is eminently helpful and indispensable!

FIELD NOTE **Getting Help with Curation**

I read blogs about new releases and recommendations to help me curate books. My most important advice comes from learners and other educators. I respect their wishes if they request a book or make a recommendation. I also communicate with other librarians frequently to get their input.

—Elizabeth Lamb (middle school librarian, Texas)

School librarians are educators first, and our first responsibility is to ensure our learners' academic achievement. When we intentionally teach our learners how to curate thoughtfully, we set them up for academic, personal, and professional success. How well we teach curation through collaboration with academic disciplines and the support of learner interests impacts their success in those pursuits. We will explore curation instruction more in depth in later chapters. For now, let us leave this chapter understanding that from the days of cave dwellers to modern times, curation has been an intricate part of establishing and maintaining civilization. We curate for learning, to enhance our lives, to document history, and to educate future generations. As the book progresses, note that curation is a natural part of being a human. Librarians do not own curation, which can take many forms depending on the setting. The collection of physical books is a small, vital portion of the essential services school librarians provide for our school communities through the Curate Shared Foundation.

Questions for the Reflective Practitioner

1. How can I gain more input from my school community about how my curation behaviors impact school-wide instruction and collaboration with colleagues?
2. How can I use the Curate Shared Foundation to shape the culture in my school community?
3. What opportunities does the Curate Shared Foundation present for me to innovate my instruction and collaborative activities?

2

Applying Curate to School Library Policy

School librarians expertly navigate and pivot between multiple roles in their daily activities as a leader, teacher, instructional partner, information specialist, and program administrator (AASL 2018). We leverage each of these roles as pillars of support when implementing policies that benefit our school communities. As leaders, we provide direction for curating materials based on the policies. As teachers, we model the best practice for curation by modeling curation as defined in the policies. In the instructional partner role, we collaboratively use the resources we have carefully selected. We activate the information specialist role when we curate resources and communicate their availability. Finally, when we are in our program administrator role, we create and implement policies.

Each of our policies affects curation and the effective use of the collection. The policies also protect the collection. For example, the selection policy reflects the standards used to choose the materials in the collection. It provides the criteria for inclusion and exclusion. We use the reconsideration policy when the quality or appropriateness of collection materials is challenged. The reconsideration policy will delineate the steps to follow to ensure that materials are kept or removed after a fair review process is implemented.

School libraries facilitate the "contribution and exchange of information within and among learning communities by establishing policies that promote effective acquisition, description, circulation, sharing, and access to resources within and beyond the school day" (AASL 2018, School Library IV.C.3.). Although school librarians in many schools and districts do this well, instances of self-censorship (Moeller and Becnel 2022) and a lack of effective policies remain (Dawkins and Eidson 2021).

Dr. April Dawkins and Emily Eidson of the University of North Carolina at Greensboro conducted a nationwide study of school library selection and reconsideration policies. Their study compared policies against a checklist adapted from the *Selection and Reconsideration Policy Toolkit for Public, School, and Academic Libraries* developed by the American Library Association (ALA) in 2018. They randomly sampled ninety-nine policies from urban, suburban, and rural districts across fifty states. Eighty policies on district websites were compared. Nineteen districts did not have policies online. Table 2.1 is adapted from the criteria derived from the toolkit used in the study.

TABLE 2.1 / **Criteria for selection and reconsideration policies in school libraries**

Foundational Information	Materials Selection	Materials Review	Reconsideration	Other Criteria
Library philosophy or mission statement	Policies and procedures for selection	Guidelines for reviewing materials and a suggested list of review sources	Reconsideration procedures	Classroom collections
Library community served	Responsibility for the selection of materials	Publication date and revision dates	Reconsideration committee guidelines/ procedures	Handling gifts and donations
Library Bill of Rights and Freedom to Read Statement	Selection objectives	Diversity of topics, authors, and opinions	Reconsideration forms	Easy to read and concise
Intellectual freedom statement and definition	Purpose of supporting curriculum and personal interests	Collection maintenance and weeding	Standing for challenges/ reconsideration	Not repetitive
	List of individual selection criteria	Age appropriateness	Controversial materials statement	Cost

The findings showed the following issues:

- Ninety percent of the policies did not mention intellectual freedom.
- Sixty percent of the policies did not mention controversy or controversial materials.
- Forty-one percent of the policies did not mention diversity.
- Twenty-six percent of the policies had not been updated in the past ten years.

School librarians, at all levels, should be intimately familiar with the policies under which they operate and should continually review them and adjust to changing conditions. Policies should be developed if they are not already in place. Policies are essential because they guide our practices and act as a shield when school library materials and programming are challenged.

Advocating for School Library Policies

A significant consideration in school librarians' curation practice is acknowledgment of the purpose of curation. Acknowledgment coincides with advocating for policies that support access to materials that interest readers. School librarians play a critical role in accessibility by highlighting deficits in collections and resources (Mackey 2022). Closely aligning work and policy development with the school's primary mission for learner achievement should drive all curation efforts. Even titles collected for pleasure reading should be considered for their widespread appeal and potential to increase self-directed reading. Ultimately, the goal is to create lifelong readers.

Advocacy can be as easy as connecting reading for pleasure to academic achievement by sharing research that proves this link. Although there have been several challenges of diverse materials in school libraries during recent years, explicitly sharing how diverse materials support teaching, the curriculum, and learning helps fortify collections against censorship attacks. For instance, research suggests that learners who read in their free time do well academically and on assessments (Whitten, Labby, and Sullivan 2019). The publications of Keith Curry Lance (n.d.) and of Keith Curry Lance and Debra E. Kachel (2018) and Scholastic's (2016) *School Libraries Work* are great places to start collecting research that provides a strong connection between learners who read widely and achieve at high levels, as well as lots of research on the impact of school library programs. AASL also provides position statements and other supporting documents for advocacy through the school library policies that support learners' growth and the Curate Shared Foundation.

FIELD NOTE **Collections Reflecting Lived Experiences**

Recently, we have seen more book challenges from the community, and I think the fear of being challenged makes many librarians self-censor. However, it has done the opposite for my closest colleagues and me. We are more determined than ever to keep a diverse collection and reflect the viewpoints of all learners. Curation in a school library is deciding what materials to purchase for the collection. It could also mean deciding which materials are outdated or irrelevant to the collection. Curation in a school library means reflecting the lived experiences of the learner population and those that may not reflect the learners' backgrounds. Curation should not reflect only the school librarian's views. It is important to curate a diverse collection that represents all learners and viewpoints they may not have considered.

—Vanessa Rivas Clouston (bilingual elementary school librarian, Texas)

Prioritizing the Learner, Not the Collection

It is essential to remember that all school library policies and procedures should exist to protect and prioritize learners. Policies should prioritize learners' access, privacy, and intellectual freedom. School library fees and fines are top obstructions to these protections and prohibit access to our curated collections. Fees and fines limit access to resources and create a barrier as school librarians work to maintain "procedures that ensure user confidentiality and promote unimpeded access to materials by staff members and learners" (AASL 2018, School Library IV.C.4.). On January 28, 2019, the ALA Council, the governing body of ALA, adopted the Resolution on Monetary Library Fines. The resolution noted that ALA opposes book fines because they are a form of social inequity. Fines present a barrier to accessing materials and prevent users from accessing up-to-date information and technology. Families with more money can pay fines. The resolution concluded with ALA establishing a working group to develop strategies and tips for assisting libraries with ending fines.

Strategies for Replacing Lost Books

Depending on your budget, losing books can be catastrophic. Still, every year, school librarians lose thousands of books. These tips will help you plan for losing books and provide options for replacing them.

1. Critically examine the lost books over the last several years. Chances are that they represent 1–2 percent of the collection each year. Library management systems can generate inventory reports. Divide the number of lost books by the number of books in the collection. For example, one hundred lost books divided by a ten-thousand-book collection equals 1 percent; one hundred lost books at $18 each equals $1,800.
2. Use the data to understand the trends in your school. Lost books are a cost of librarianship. Allocate a portion of the budget for replacements.
3. Use data to advocate for additional funding to replace lost items for the school library.
4. Get the community involved in replacement efforts by asking community groups, local businesses, and social media contacts for donations.
5. Ask your advisory group for fund-raising ideas and then communicate with the parent-teacher organization (PTO) to support the fund-raising goals.
6. Share information with PTO members, other educators, and administrators about the inequity of fees and fines. Use the data you have collected and incorporate stories of learners who could not pay and have lost access to the school library, sometimes for years, as a result.
7. During school library orientation, or the first few school year lessons, emphasize that not returning or caring for school library books hurts the learning community. When a book is lost or damaged beyond repair, privately speak with the learner. When appropriate, gently ask if they can return or replace the book so that others can enjoy it. Let them know they are a valuable community member who is still welcome to borrow school library materials.
8. Review communication about overdue books. Revise messages to include friendly reminders instead of threats.
9. Host a bookfair and consider using the resulting funds to replace the books.
10. Create a Birthday Book Club. Parents can donate a book to honor their child's birthday. Add a bookplate inside the book with the child's name and the year. Keep a list of books that you need and their prices. Alternatively, ask parents to donate the average book cost and then you order the book. Always follow your selection policy guidelines.

Developing Selection Policies

Given their importance, creating a selection policy can seem daunting. ALA has created materials to assist. However, it is good to understand how the examples provided by ALA can be adapted for school libraries. The following is an example of a district collection policy incorporating the ALA (2018) recommendations. The policy emphasizes creating diverse collections. Italicized items specifically support diversity, inclusion, and equity.

ABC School District

The ABC School District reaffirms the American Library Association's Interpretation of the Library Bill of Rights for "Access to Resources and Services in the School Library." It asserts that the school library has the following responsibilities:

1. To provide intellectual and physical access to resources in appropriate formats.
2. To provide a comprehensive collection of instructional materials that comply with basic written selection principles and provide maximum accessibility to these materials.
3. To provide materials for educators and learners to stimulate growth in knowledge, literary appreciation, and aesthetic values.
4. To provide materials that will enrich and support the curriculum, considering the varied interests, abilities, and maturity levels of learners served.
5. To provide materials in an appropriate and current format to effectively teach the curriculum.
6. To provide materials that will stimulate growth in factual knowledge, literary appreciation, aesthetic values, and ethical standards.
7. To provide a background of information that will enable learners to make intelligent judgments in their daily lives.
8. To provide materials on opposing sides of controversial issues so that young citizens may develop the practice of critical analysis of all media under guidance.
9. *To provide materials reflective of the pluralistic nature of a global society.*
10. To place principle above personal opinion and avoid prejudice in selecting materials of the highest quality to ensure a comprehensive collection appropriate for the school library users.
11. To anticipate and meet needs through awareness of subjects of current interest.
12. To provide materials with a recent copyright date as appropriate to the subject.

13. *To ensure that all bilingual programs have a diverse and wide range of materials available.*

At no time will the wishes of one learner's parents or guardians to restrict their reading or viewing of a particular item infringe on other parents' or guardians' rights to permit their child to read or view the same material.

SELECTION CRITERIA

Materials should be thoughtfully selected based on several criteria:

- Educational and curricular significance of the subject matter
- Purpose and potential usefulness of the materials
- Appropriateness of the subject for the age, ability level, learning style, and social and emotional development of the learners for whom the materials are selected
- *Cultural responsiveness: materials that represent the many cultures, religions, sexual orientations, gender identities, and ethnic groups that comprise our school community and society*
- *Ability to engage learners, facilitating student agency and reading motivation*
- *Represent a variety of viewpoints*
- Provide information on all sides of issues
- Ability to motivate learners, educators, and staff to examine their attitudes, behaviors, responsibilities, rights, and privileges as members of our community and to make informed decisions in their daily lives
- Offer a range of reading levels
- *Minimum of two positive reviews from respected professional journals or evaluation tools such as* The Horn Book, Kirkus Reviews, School Library Journal, Booklist, *or We Need Diverse Books (Diversebooks.org)*
- *Local and national media awards and recommended lists such as the Newbery, Caldecott, Coretta Scott King Book Awards, and IBBY Honour List*
- Validity, currency, accuracy, and developmental appropriateness
- *Meet the language needs of the community*
- Attractiveness and appeal of illustrations, graphics, and format

DONATIONS

- Book donations must meet the same criteria as book purchases.
- The school library accepts donations of materials from the community with no stipulations from the donor.
- The donor understands that the school librarian is free to decide whether all or part of the gift or donation should be integrated into the collection or discarded.
- A plan to eliminate unwanted donations is clearly incorporated into the policy.

Ensuring Diversity in Curated Resources

School libraries provide "an environment in which resources that support the school's curriculum and learning goals can be collaboratively selected and developed" (AASL 2018, School Library IV.C.1.). Policies should ensure that school librarians represent diverse identities and viewpoints, especially unpopular or marginalized identities and viewpoints. According to ALA's (2019) interpretation of the Library Bill of Rights, "a diverse collection should contain content by and about a wide array of people and cultures to authentically reflect a variety of ideas, information, stories, and experiences." In keeping with these suggestions, use announcements, newsletters, class presentations, and one-to-one conversations to inform learners that collections reflect diverse populations and viewpoints. Using multiple, creditable sources of reviews and recommendations for collection input is also essential.

AASL advocates for "designing opportunities for learners to explore possible information sources" (AASL 2018, School Librarian IV.A.2.). Reach beyond the familiar sources of information to learn about current social issues and movements, then embrace increased diversity in your collection and your collection-development habits. For example, become familiar with We Need Diverse Books, A Mighty Girl, and Debbie Reese's blog *American Indians in Children's Literature* about outstanding books by and about Native Americans. Finally, establish a library advisory committee and take part in professional learning networks to understand new texts and materials. Learners are far more likely to access and use collections that reflect their interests.

DIVERSITY AUDITS

Diversity audits are a powerful practice rooted in equity. The school librarian undertakes a close, critical examination of the items in the school library to ensure that the collection reflects, supports, and empowers learners and the community. Most of us assume that we are creating an inclusive collection. However, we must leave our comfort zone to analyze our collection-development practices. As Karen Jensen (2018) explained, "A diversity audit takes inventory and determines what's in a collection and what areas need to be better developed. It yields concrete data. This type of audit helps put the *science* in *library science*" (italics in original). Specifically, diversity audits help school librarians acknowledge their societal privileges and how that worldview influences collection development.

Diversity audits begin with research. Jensen's initial research included collecting baseline data, which reflected U.S. census information. She also used lists from We Need Diverse Books and data from the Cooperative Children's Book Center, and she read Lee & Low's Diversity Baseline Survey to understand publishing culture and how it relates to developing inclusive collections.

Her next step was to analyze her collection using an Excel spreadsheet. She reviewed each title to determine "whether the title involved characters who were something other than male, white, nondisabled, and heteronormative." The data were then used to target areas that needed more attention. Jensen described the process as time-consuming but worth it. We encourage you to explore her article more. She provides tips for performing small diversity audits when a full diversity audit is impossible because of time constraints. Conducting a diversity audit can be an excellent professional development exercise, summer project, or learning opportunity for school librarianship practicum students. The benefits of putting ourselves and our collections to this test far outweigh any potential discomfort we may feel as we learn what we have and don't have for our learners and community at a new level.

Similarly, Sandra Hughes-Hassell (2020) recommended collecting specific diversity data about learners. She used a form to collect the details for each book and then analyzed the results. Like Jensen (2018), Hughes-Hassell asserted that diversity audits make collection development a data-driven practice that can reflect the school's population and needs.

Key Components of Data-Driven Diversity Audits

When auditing your collection for diversity, log each book title and barcode and then record the following information for each book or story:

- Economics (Wealthy, Middle Class, Low Income)
- Religion
- Main Character(s) Characteristics (LGBTQIA+, Race, Ethnicity, Disability, Other)
- Main Character(s) Gender
- Author's Race or Ethnicity

You can add other elements to your audit—for example, mental health, immigrant/refugee status, and more.

Hughes-Hassell explained that diverse characters or stories do not need to focus on stereotypical situations or feature struggling characters. Conducting a diversity audit and subsequently adjusting collection-development and management practices and procedures are excellent examples of "using local and external data to inform ongoing adjustments to the scope of the resource collection, and its audiences, formats, and applications" (AASL 2018, School Library IV.D.4.).

AVOIDING THE STATUS QUO

Failing to ensure collection diversity supports the status quo. In March 2022, the ALA Council passed the "Resolution to Promote Equity, Diversity, and Inclusion (EDI) Efforts in AASL While Addressing Historical Effects of Racism." The resolution's text noted that "equity, diversity, and inclusion are within every area of school librarian practice, including collection development, professional development, recruiting, mentoring, and instruction through our *National School Library Standards*" (ALA Council 2022a). Addressing the importance of this resolution, Diane Chen, AASL Division Councilor, explained that AASL took several steps to rectify past actions that disenfranchised minorities. Chen (2022) made the following statement:

> At a time when school and youth librarians are being targeted in our society for our intellectual freedom and social justice efforts; at a time when our BIPOC students are losing equitable access to school librarians and their libraries; at a time when we need to be standing together, taking action and communicating to others, this is when ALA needs to join with us to acknowledge the past, commit to doing better, and sharing our message of power and hope to promote Equity, Diversity, and Inclusion Efforts in ALA while addressing historical effects of racism.

The resolution was a call to action. One need look no further than Melvil Dewey's behavior and the history of library participation in segregation and elitist policies to see that the status quo must be challenged if school libraries are to remain relevant (Wheeler, Johnson-Houston, and Walker 2004). School library programming and collections should accurately reflect society. Inclusiveness extends beyond curated digital resources and books. Consider the authors and storytellers who visit, the books that vendors include in bookfairs, and the selection and retention of resources in school curricula. School librarians are responsible for "employing a dynamic collection policy that includes selection and retention criteria for all materials within the collection" (AASL 2018, School Library IV.B.3.) and for ensuring that all curation activities undertaken by our schools are inclusive.

Navigating Material Challenges

School librarians promote information gathering appropriate to the task by "implementing an administratively approved and endorsed policy that clearly addresses procedures for handling material challenges" (AASL 2018, School Library IV.B.4.). Being prepared to respond to challenges is one way that school librarians can exemplify this skill. Collection development and providing access to materials are fundamental constructs for implementing an exceptional school library program. Prepared school librarians can point to organized documentation that relates selected materials to the school curriculum (Philippi and Calzada 2022). They use a systematic structure for reviewing materials to add to the collection.

FIELD NOTE

Policies for Curation and Collection Development

Recently, school library collections have been politicized. This behavior has forced us to reexamine our collections and our policies for curation and collection development. To address this issue, as a certified, trained professional librarian, I have the skills to evaluate what meets the curation standards set forth by our school district. When a specific item's place in the collection is called into question, we have procedures in place for reviewing the item for reconsideration.

—Dawn Fontana (elementary school librarian, Texas)

Material challenges are a reality in school libraries. Mary Jo Godwin has been credited with saying, "A truly great library has something in it to offend everyone." School libraries need a policy clearly stating how material challenges will be handled. Frequently, the policy is developed by the district. Following the selection and challenge policy and ensuring that the school community knows it exists are essential. For example, copies can be distributed to new educators, copies can be kept in the school library, and the policy should be placed on the library's website.

In 2022, principals, superintendents, school board members, and other educators increasingly unilaterally removed books from classrooms and school libraries without following established policies and procedures. Connolly (2022) noted that many of these challenges began after the Leander Independent School District in Texas attempted to support student choice of book clubs with diverse reading materials in English language arts classrooms. Although the books were not required reading, challenges to the books soon began, resulting in the removal of eleven books from classrooms. Challenges soon swept the nation.

FIELD NOTE **Communicating with Parents**

At the beginning of my career, I had a couple of parents try to get a book removed from the school library system. Most parents, in finding they need to read the entire book in order to start the process, will decide not to go through with it. Our district has a policy for that, so I spoke with the parents and let them know what they would need to do. The one time a parent challenged the book, a committee was formed at the district level, the book was reviewed, the parent's challenge was considered, and the book was not removed.

—Trina Samson (elementary school librarian, Washington)

The increase in these cases prompted Dr. Joyce Valenza, professor and former school librarian, to lead the development of the ALA Council's (2022b) "Resolution to Support School and Youth Services Librarians Facing Increased Intellectual Freedom Challenges." According to the resolution, school librarians are facing unprecedented calls for dismissal based on the content of library collections. The resolution further states ALA's commitment "to ongoing support of all children's right to read . . . by . . . upholding a parent's right to decide what their own children can read, but not what other children can read as stated in the *Access to Library Resources and Services for Minors: An Interpretation of the Library Bill of Rights* and the *Access to Resources and Services in the School Library*." Finally, the resolution notes that school librarians should "follow board-approved policies and procedures, selecting and maintaining collections that are age-appropriate, high quality, and balanced to meet curricular and personal interests, and promote student choice." Well-defined policies state the steps that need to be followed for challenges and provide examples of correspondence that can be distributed. Consistently following well-defined selection and challenge policies can save school librarians from being prosecuted. Always remain professional, impartial, and, as much as possible, dispassionate throughout the process. In addition, remember that the ALA Office for Intellectual Freedom and the Freedom to Read Foundation provide confidential support.

Digital Resources and Privacy

Digital curation has become an integral part of collection development. Digital resources should follow collection guidelines similar to those for print sources, and many digital tools are available for curating collections. The AASL (2021) position statement "The Critical Need for and Responsibilities of District-Level School Library Supervisors" notes that a district-level supervisor "guides and promotes adherence to policies and procedures regarding intellectual property, privacy, and digital citizenship in accordance with the district's code of ethics." However, some school districts do not have district-level supervisors for school librarians. As a result, when we curate digital resources such as apps, websites, and other tools for our learners, we must also ensure that we align our work with school, district, and board policies. Then we must further align with state and local laws and federal laws such as the Family Educational Rights and Privacy Act (FERPA) and the Americans with Disabilities Act (ADA). Consider your learners' data, how their privacy is protected, how their information is shared with other companies, and the prospect of data breaches. School libraries must work to maintain "procedures that ensure user confidentiality and promote unimpeded access to materials by staff members and learners" (AASL 2018, School Library IV.C.4.).

Sample Policy and Procedure for Challenged Materials

A learner (in this case, a student), parent, employee, or district resident may formally challenge instructional materials based on appropriateness. A parent's ability to exercise control over reading, listening to, or viewing matter is limited to their own children. When materials are challenged, the freedom to read, view, and listen to diverse materials should be defended. The final decision on challenged materials is based on the appropriateness of the material for its intended instructional use. No challenged school library material will be removed solely because of the ideas expressed in the material.

INFORMAL REQUEST FOR RECONSIDERATION

The school receiving a complaint should try to resolve concerns regarding appropriateness in the following manner: the school librarian or principal will explain the school's selection process and the role of the questionable material in the educational program.

FORMAL REQUEST FOR RECONSIDERATION

If the complainant wishes to make a formal challenge, the following process will be followed:

1. The school librarian will provide a copy of the "Request for Reconsideration" form and a copy of the selection policy (see ALA's *Selection and Reconsideration Policy Toolkit for Public, School, and Academic Libraries*) and then notify the principal within the same day.
2. Access to the challenged material will be restricted (e.g., limited to access with parental permission) during the reconsideration process.
3. Upon receipt of the form, the principal will form a committee. An example of a reconsideration committee may include a district administrator, a librarian from the school district who is not at the school with the challenged material, an administrator from the school, a classroom educator from the school, and the school librarian.
4. All members of the committee must review the material in its entirety. The committee will evaluate the material based on its entirety rather than on passages or selections taken out of context. The committee will prepare a written report for the complainant and the superintendent.

APPEAL PROCESS

The complainant may appeal the decision of the reconsideration committee formed by the school principal. The appeal should contain

- a copy of the original complaint,
- the reconsideration committee's report, and
- the dates of all meetings regarding the request for reconsideration.

These materials are submitted to the school district for review by a committee established by the superintendent or their designee.

Fortunately, several resources can help. First, consider whether the resource provider is a signatory to the Student Privacy Pledge, a movement by educational technology companies to commit to protecting student data privacy (Future of Privacy Forum and Software and Information Industry Association, n.d.). We can hold vendors with whom we work to the commitments in this pledge and serve as a strong voice in ensuring learner privacy. Data security is one of the primary considerations when doing business with these entities. Not only can the Student Privacy Pledge help you research whether a resource you are considering protects student privacy, but you may even find new resources you have not heard of before.

Next, consider that everyone needs to protect their privacy. Companies are learning everything there is to know about us by accessing online profiles. Our learners are creating profiles of themselves online with every search they undertake, every link they click, and every online resource they view. The information we unwittingly provide companies about our preferences, tastes, and activities is sold, transferred, and traded. Information is power, and our personal information is one of the most valuable assets that the companies with whom we interact have about us. We owe it to our learners to shield them from unscrupulous service providers who harvest their personal information and to teach them about what is happening behind the scenes when they use a commercial search engine, shop online, view videos, or otherwise interact with content.

Large companies such as Illuminate Education, Pearson, Naviance, and K12 have had large data breaches in the past several years (Kuykendall 2022; Schwarz 2020), exposing personally identifiable information (PII) of thousands of current and former students to hackers. Schools and districts must do a better job of securing student PII, and school librarians have an essential role in advocating for student data privacy in policy and instruction.

A Final Word on School Library Policies

Our responsibilities under the School Library Alignments of the Curate Shared Foundation call for school librarians to examine school library policies and procedures. School librarians must ensure that, at a minimum, collection-development and reconsideration policies are in place for building and district levels. If these policies are not in place or are out of date, access ALA and AASL examples and seek guidance from your PLNs to write or update them. Then set a schedule to revisit and revise school library policies at least every few years. In addition, ensure that a solid privacy policy is in place while teaching learners the skills needed to protect their personal information.

Include school community stakeholders such as administrators, other educators, and learners in developing policies so that they will endorse them. Once the policies have been written or revised, communicate with your school community about accessing the policies. Developing a powerful community of advocates will go a long way as you work to implement and maintain the established policies.

Questions for the Reflective Practitioner

1. What school library policies do I have in place that may need to be updated or may be missing?
2. As I consider the data or supporting literature that I can share, what policies will I review first? How will I communicate the importance of these policies?
3. Who in my learning community could be a potential ally in developing, advocating for, and implementing new policies in my school or district?

PART II

Curation for Learners

3

Teaching Learners to Curate

School librarians are teachers first and are called to provide explicit curation instruction to learners, as stated in the Curate Shared Foundation. The primary responsibility is to ensure that learners leave school ready to take on the challenging, ever-transforming information landscape as independent, lifelong learners. The *National School Library Standards* reflect long-standing best practices in curation for school libraries and offer opportunities for school librarians to grow professionally and be innovative leaders who curate outside traditional collection-development practices. The Curate Shared Foundation is the key to school librarianship because most school librarian professional activities revolve around the collection of resources for learners.

Great school libraries are far more than their collections. It is possible to be a terrific school librarian without having a robust, current, and relevant collection. However, the collection is central to integrating the library program into the school community, instruction with learners, and collaborations with other educators (Krutka 2022). It is essential to make collection development, and modeling and teaching curation outside the traditional school library collection, a priority. The Learner Competencies under the Curate Shared Foundation provide a roadmap to ensure that learners become curators. The opportunities for learners to practice acting on an information need, gathering information appropriate to the task, exchanging information within and beyond the school, and selecting and organizing information for various audiences are limited only by imagination! Of course, excellent curation work begins in the center of our school library operation—the collection.

Building a Foundation for Instruction Using Pre-Assessment

Gathering information about prior knowledge before teaching learners or staff about curation and resources or providing any instruction is useful. Formal pre-assessment of staff members' and learners' knowledge of resources is ideal for differentiating instruction. However, it often is not practical to administer assessments and analyze results before last-minute instruction requests. School librarians frequently conduct informal pre-assessments on the fly by talking with educator partners about their needs and understanding of learners' resource knowledge. Quick polls or question-and-answer periods to start a lesson or professional development session are helpful when a conversation isn't feasible. For instance, using Kahoot! and other gamified quiz results can quickly identify learners' level of knowledge about resources before starting a lesson. Before lessons, consider developing a few questions to determine learners' amount of background knowledge. Responses will reveal whether a group has had instruction on the distinction between search engines and databases. Try these questions about subscription databases.

1. What is the difference between a database and a search engine like Google?
   a. There is no difference; they work the same.
   b. Databases are paid for by the school and do not contain ads.
   c. Google searches *everything* on the Internet.
   d. Databases focus on academic content.
   e. Both b and d are correct.

2. List at least three databases that the school library provides.

3. You can save the citations for the materials you find in a database in the following way(s):
   a. Word Document
   b. Google Document
   c. RefWorks
   d. NoodleTools
   e. All of the above

4. The information in a database has been checked for accuracy and credibility.
   a. True
   b. False

An advantage of using questions as quick pre-assessments is that they can become conversation starters. Conversations often center on real-life applications of the skills that are being demonstrated. These connections make the instruction meaningful and relatable. Furthermore, school-age learners can also benefit significantly from a pre-assessment to determine their knowledge of information source types. Elementary learners can often differentiate between stories, articles, videos, and various formats and genres. If they can't, teachable moments can be woven into the school library introduction lessons.

Also remember that acting on pre-assessments is not the only way to plan for teaching curation skills. First, consider the needs of your school community. For example, you can coordinate with other school librarians in your district, region, or state. Then take part in a collaborative session with them to determine what learners at specific grade levels should know and be able to do relevant to Curate and all the Shared Foundations. Our colleagues in Texas have done tremendous work on a school library standards document that aligns the 2018 Texas School Library Program Standards with a variety of national standards, including AASL's *National School Library Standards* (Texas State Library and Archives Commission, n.d.). Their alignments also include crosswalks with the International Society for Technology in Education (ISTE) and the Association of College and Research Libraries (ACRL). The crosswalks provide an excellent opportunity to grasp how the *National School Library Standards* relate to technology implementation and college preparation from a state viewpoint. If your state or district has not yet developed a similar document, check with your PLN online and the other states in your region. We're sure you will discover other great examples of alignment as you consider which curation competencies your learners need to build.

Developing Competent Curators through the Domains

How can educators connect learners to the Curate Shared Foundation? What should learners know to be deemed competent curators? In the following sections, we will delve into these questions by considering the skills that learners should know. Ultimately, these skills or competencies will help with planning lessons. Plan lessons to assist learners with making meaning for themselves "and others by collecting, organizing, and sharing resources of personal relevance" (AASL 2018, 37).

Learning trajectories (tables 3.1, 3.2, and 3.3 on the following pages) have been provided to demonstrate the Competencies that learners exhibit through the Curate Shared Foundation. The charts for the upper grades assume the skills taught in the lower grade levels. The text is not all-inclusive because learners must develop other skills. However, the trajectories present starting points for scaffolding learning within Curate. After reading this chapter, you may find the learning trajectories and the lesson plan starters in the appendix helpful for conceptualizing each Domain.

TABLE 3.1 / **Curate learning trajectory: Kindergarten–fourth grade**

THINK **Learners act on an information need by:**	**CREATE** **Learners gather information appropriate to the task by:**
Learner IV.A.1. Determining the need to gather information. With assistance, learners can: • Articulate what they already know and want to know about a topic • Create questions about a topic of interest **Learner IV.A.2. Identifying possible sources of information.** With assistance, learners can: • Discuss the difference between a nonfiction and fiction resource • Use question words (who, what, when, where, and how) to identify materials for research **Learner IV.A.3. Making critical choices about information sources to use.** With assistance, learners can: • Articulate the difference between facts and opinions • Identify the main topic, key events, and each character's purpose in stories or informational texts • Utilize feedback on projects to engage in the inquiry process	**Learner IV.B.1. Seeking a variety of sources.** With assistance, learners can: • Describe their information need to school librarians and teachers • Identify informational resources such as websites, books, newspapers, magazines, databases, and audiovisual materials **Learner IV.B.2. Collecting information representing diverse perspectives.** With assistance, learners can: • Listen to other learners to create new meaning • Identify the main topic, point of view, and important details from texts **Learner IV.B.3. Systematically questioning and assessing the validity and accuracy of information.** With assistance, learners can: • Use question words (who, what, when, where, and how) to identify differences in texts • Utilize charts, data, graphs, diagrams, and timelines from texts to support conclusions **Learner IV.B.4. Organizing information by priority, topic, or other systematic scheme.** With assistance, learners can: • Generate and answer follow-up questions to clarify the meaning of information • Review informational materials and create an informational resource to share an opinion in a logical order (i.e., introduction, discussion, and conclusion)

SHARE

Learners exchange information resources within and beyond their learning community by:

Learner IV.C.1. Accessing and evaluating collaboratively constructed information sites.

With assistance, learners can:

- Collaborate with other learners to solve problems based on the information found or presented
- Accept and provide feedback about projects with other learners

Learner IV.C.2. Contributing to collaboratively constructed information sites by ethically using and reproducing others' work.

With assistance, learners can:

- Contribute to class discussions
- Exchange ideas in the form of texts, video or audio recordings, drawings, or charts with other learners

Learner IV.C.3. Joining with others to compare and contrast information derived from collaboratively constructed information sites.

With assistance, learners can:

- Ask and answer questions about text details in a group setting to gain a deeper understanding of a topic during discussions
- Identify the similarities and differences between information resources using features such as pictures, text, titles, main characters, and points of view

GROW

Learners select and organize information for a variety of audiences by:

Learner IV.D.1. Performing ongoing analysis of and reflection on the quality, usefulness, and accuracy of curated resources.

With assistance, learners can:

- Identify the differences in the information presented in texts (i.e., title, captions, glossary, index, author, pictures)
- Assess the benefits of using different types of information sources

Learner IV.D.2. Integrating and depicting in a conceptual knowledge network their understanding gained from resources.

With assistance, learners can:

- Describe the connection between people, places, things, events, and texts
- Remember a conversation from a previous lesson and continue the discussion during the next class session

Learner IV.D.3. Openly communicating curation processes for others to use, interpret, and validate.

With assistance, learners can:

- Discuss conflicting information
- Support their ideas with information that they have gathered

Source: Developed by Daniella LaShaun Smith for *Curate,* part IV in the Shared Foundations series.

TABLE 3.2 / **Curate learning trajectory: Fifth–eighth grades**

THINK **Learners act on an information need by:**	**CREATE** **Learners gather information appropriate to the task by:**
Learner IV.A.1. Determining the need to gather information. Learners can: • Recall prior knowledge to identify knowledge gaps to gather information • Design research questions to study a topic	**Learner IV.B.1. Seeking a variety of sources.** Learners can: • Find additional resources to support an author's point of view • Seek information in different formats to develop a rich understanding of a topic
Learner IV.A.2. Identifying possible sources of information. Learners can: • Examine print, audiovisual, and digital sources to determine their appropriateness for supporting research • Identify individuals to interview to answer research questions	**Learner IV.B.2. Collecting information representing diverse perspectives.** Learners can: • Integrate information from diverse texts to draw conclusions • Summarize and paraphrase information gathered from multiple texts
Learner IV.A.3. Making critical choices about information sources to use. Learners can: • Choose information in a variety of formats, including graphics, audio recordings, text, and videos • Determine the purpose of a text and how the purpose is conveyed	**Learner IV.B.3. Systematically questioning and assessing the validity and accuracy of information.** Learners can: • Provide evidence from credible sources to support points in texts • Implement lateral reading to analyze texts
	Learner IV.B.4. Organizing information by priority, topic, or other systematic scheme. Learners can: • Arrange information from several sources to create a cohesive report or speech • Provide a presentation in a logical format that includes an introduction, a summary of facts, opinions based on facts, and a conclusion

SHARE **Learners exchange information resources within and beyond their learning community by:**	**GROW** **Learners select and organize information for a variety of audiences by:**
Learner IV.C.1. Accessing and evaluating collaboratively constructed information sites. Learners can: • Add to and utilize the information in a blog, wiki, or discussion board • Evaluate the usefulness of information on collaborative blogs, wikis, or discussion boards to draw conclusions and synthesize new knowledge	**Learner IV.D.1. Performing ongoing analysis of and reflection on the quality, usefulness, and accuracy of curated resources.** Learners can: • Utilize prior and new knowledge to determine the usefulness of information • Apply lateral thinking to determine the accuracy and usefulness of resources
Learner IV.C.2. Contributing to collaboratively constructed information sites by ethically using and reproducing others' work. Learners can: • Interpret and apply copyright and fair use guidelines • Understand and apply digital citizenship concepts	**Learner IV.D.2. Integrating and depicting in a conceptual knowledge network their understanding gained from resources.** Learners can: • Applying critical thinking skills during discussions to analyze information • Create and articulate new meaning from information gathered during discussions
Learner IV.C.3. Joining with others to compare and contrast information derived from collaboratively constructed information sites. Learners can: • Use documentation from literature and nonfiction texts to address research questions on a class blog • Compare and contrast texts with other learners to determine if biased and conflicting information is presented	**Learner IV.D.3. Openly communicating curation processes for others to use, interpret, and validate.** Learners can: • Deliver speeches and presentations demonstrating their understanding of research topics • Respond to questions asked about the information-seeking process and source validity

Source: Developed by Daniella LaShaun Smith for *Curate,* part IV in the Shared Foundations series.

TABLE 3.3 / **Curate learning trajectory: Ninth–twelfth grades**

THINK **Learners act on an information need by:**	**CREATE** **Learners gather information appropriate to the task by:**
Learner IV.A.1. Determining the need to gather information. Learners can: • Complete a schematic map to identify keywords and synonyms relevant to a research question • Formulate new research questions based on information that has been gathered	**Learner IV.B.1. Seeking a variety of sources.** Learners can: • Locate sources of information in multiple formats (digital, print, text, audiovisual) • Create surveys and interview questions • Identify participants for surveys and interviews
Learner IV.A.2. Identifying possible sources of information. Learners can: • Use a reference list to determine new sources of information to use • Use a database and seek information identified in the database as similar to the current resource	**Learner IV.B.2. Collecting information representing diverse perspectives.** Learners can: • Identify divergent viewpoints and investigate sources related to each viewpoint • Implement surveys and perform member checking to clarify viewpoints presented
Learner IV.A.3. Making critical choices about information sources to use. Learners can: • Use deductive reasoning to identify sources of information that present malicious intent • Strategically select digital media to enhance a presentation	**Learner IV.B.3. Systematically questioning and assessing the validity and accuracy of information.** Learners can: • Use comparative analysis to determine whether discrepancies exist in data and other sources of information • Provide and cite justifications for decisions made about sources of information
	Learner IV.B.4. Organizing information by priority, topic, or other systematic scheme. Learners can: • Plan, outline, organize, and edit an in-depth research paper • Create organized infographics to communicate findings based on a given task

SHARE

Learners exchange information resources within and beyond their learning community by:

Learner IV.C.1. Accessing and evaluating collaboratively constructed information sites.

Learners can:

- Access the information presented by a group and determine the knowledge gaps in the project
- Review collaboratively produced materials to determine if contradictions exist and further questions and answers needed to resolve them

Learner IV.C.2. Contributing to collaboratively constructed information sites by ethically using and reproducing others' work.

Learners can:

- Select and apply appropriate Creative Commons licenses
- Use a specific citing style (e.g., APA, MLA, Turabian)

Learner IV.C.3. Joining with others to compare and contrast information derived from collaboratively constructed information sites.

Learners can:

- Formulate a plan during group work to determine how to answer questions presented by a knowledge gap
- Collect and share data on a wiki, blog, or repository for others to use and analyze

GROW

Learners select and organize information for a variety of audiences by:

Learner IV.D.1. Performing ongoing analysis of and reflection on the quality, usefulness, and accuracy of curated resources.

Learners can:

- Consider cultural and social contexts when interpreting the quality of sources
- Collaboratively create and implement a rubric to determine the quality, usefulness, and accuracy of curated resources

Learner IV.D.2. Integrating and depicting in a conceptual knowledge network their understanding gained from resources.

Learners can:

- Prepare responses for a debate by discussing divergent viewpoints
- Explain to a group of peers or adults how an event unfolds over time

Learner IV.D.3. Openly communicating curation processes for others to use, interpret, and validate.

Learners can:

- Develop a research plan, collect data, and write and post a research paper that uses qualitative or quantitative data, or both, for peer review
- Use technology to publish, revise, and update resources based on feedback

Source: Developed by Daniella LaShaun Smith for *Curate,* part IV in the Shared Foundations series.

Think

Learners act on an information need by determining the need to gather information (Learner IV.A.1.). School librarians help learners see the value in gathering authoritative information instead of Googling for quick answers. Developing an aptitude for carefully gathering content will help learners make connections that deepen their understanding of a topic or task. Building a sense of urgency about the need to gather information is a characteristic of good teaching. Good teaching involves tapping into learners' interests and curiosity, encouraging them to become excited about asking questions and searching for answers. Emphasize curated collections, such as academic databases, resources curated by you, or resources that you have linked to from other school librarians and educators.

Curated resources will not meet every need. Therefore, teaching the school community how to use commercial search engines effectively is important because learners need to understand that the first results that appear are not guaranteed to be the best or most accurate (Mignardi 2021). Teach learners to select search keywords and implement searches. Coach them in common search engine Boolean operators, such as quotation marks, wildcards, and limiters. Demonstrate advanced search and filters to help learners tame the information overload that Google searching often presents. Dive into resources like Google Scholar and Wikipedia, which are often criticized by educators but loved by youth. Explain that those resources are terrific starting points for locating sources and hard-to-find information on various topics.

Learners act on an information need by identifying possible sources of information (Learner IV.A.2.). As learners begin the research process, school librarians teach them to look for and start recognizing subject experts—namely, those whose works keep appearing in learners' search results and the bibliographies of their sources. Teach learners to track these people and their work to learn about their contributions. Prompt learners to find out about organizations that are involved with the topic. Through this investigation, learners will learn about interested parties, both public and private, profit-making and charitable, and their motivations. As an illustration, secondary learners enjoy learning to follow the money on specific issues to determine who profits from the status quo and who stands to lose if a change occurs.

When learners identify potential sources of information, work with them to understand resource formats, their potential purposes, audiences, strengths, and limitations. Guide learners toward professionally curated resources specific to the task at hand. Such instruction for middle school and older learners emphasizes how Google and other search engines create revenue by gathering targeted user information to sell to other companies. Google and other companies are in the advertising business, not the search business (Graham 2017).

Learners act on an information need by making critical choices about information sources to use (Learner IV.A.3.). As learners delve deeper into topics, school librarians teach them to apply frameworks and skills for evaluating their sources. These methods include the RADAR (Relevance, Authority, Date, Appearance, Reason) Framework (Mandalios 2013) and the SIFT (Stop, Investigate, Find, Trace) process (Caulfield 2017), which help learners implement lateral reading. Learners should inspect sources, moving beyond accepting information at face value to question the motives behind the work. Ask learners to study texts with attention to the author's or creator's purpose and way of expressing their opinions.

Freedom of speech means everyone gets to express themselves. However, it does not mean that every idea deserves equal consideration or any consideration at all. Thinking for ourselves is hard work that requires the critical evaluation of concepts. Evaluation determines the ideas worthy of our attention and the dismissal of potentially threatening opinions. Methods for making these determinations exist, but they are not helpful if they are not taught (Axford 2018). Figures 3.1 and 3.2 demonstrate how to use each framework for questioning and assessing the validity and accuracy of information.

R — Relevance

- Is the document applicable to your research questions?
- Is the information in the document specifically related to your task?
- Who was the information written for?
- Will the document help you with your task?

A — Authority

- Who created the resource?
- Why is the person or organization who created the resource qualified to discuss the topic?
- Is there a better source that is more qualified to address the topic?

D — Date

- Does the document have a date?
- Based on the date, is the information in the document too old to be used for your project?
- Should you find information that is more up to date?

A — Appearance

- Does the document look professional or scholarly?
- Are references to support the document included and have you checked them?
- Is there anything in the document, such as an advertisement, that suggests that you should not use it?

R — Reason

- Why was the document written?
- Is the document neutral or is it designed to persuade you, to teach you, or to sell a product?
- Does the document seem to be biased?

FIGURE 3.1 / **RADAR Framework questions**

S — Stop

Don't end your search with the first source that you find. Search engines often sort relevant information further down in the results. Stop and review the source. In this step, you do not need to read the source. Instead, ask yourself if you are familiar with the source of information. Do you know the reputation of the person, organization, or company? If not, you should not waste your time reading or sharing it until you know where the information originated. Now move to the next step in the process.

I — Investigate

It is time to investigate to determine if the material is from a reputable source. The reputation may be evaluated by examining the author to determine if they have the requisite knowledge to write the content. For instance, a researcher with an established reputation for publishing in peer-reviewed journals about a topic is likely a better source than a mystery writer on the Internet. The same is true of articles that are found in databases provided by the school. Moreover, the website URL can provide important information regarding its purpose. Examine the URL to determine if it is a .co, .com, .edu, .gov, .org, or .net.

F — Find

Sometimes media will be written by a lesser-known person or organization. However, it may have the potential to be correct. In that case, you need to find out if it represents a popular viewpoint about a topic. In this case, you will need to find the best source for the topic. Look at multiple sources that have been shared by experts or well documented. You may not share the viewpoint. However, it just needs to be documented well.

T — Trace

In this step, look at the documentation and trace it back to its origin. Investigate the citations and links included in the source. What was the original context for the information that has been shared? Is there something missing from what has been written or shared in a recording or video? What does the original content say about the topic? Is the information in the source that you found misleading based on your analysis of the original information? Asking yourself these questions will enable you to understand the original intent of the information and accurately represent it yourself.

FIGURE 3.2 / **Steps in the SIFT process**

Encourage your learners to use at least one of these frameworks each time they review information. In addition, teach your learners about the meaning of a peer-reviewed article and the differences between website domains. For example, a .edu or .gov site is likely to be more credible than a .net or .com website. Moreover, a website such as TinEye will provide a reverse image search to assist learners in determining whether a website has stolen or photoshopped images.

Create

Learners gather information appropriate to the task by seeking a variety of sources (Learner IV.B.1.). Databases can help learners curate various resources focused on academic subjects. Databases are an excellent place to start information gathering and are likely available through public, academic, and school libraries via statewide or regional licensing cooperatives. Check with your state library, department of education, or other state-level entities to determine whether databases are available. Be sure to regularly share links, authentication information, and extensive instructions on using databases. For example, QR codes linking to databases and other resources can be placed on posters throughout the school library.

When learners are accessing database articles, they must understand that database providers are not the authors but simply the curators of these articles. Resources from databases represent multiple news outlets, academic journals, e-books, and other types of sources. The resources in databases are often curated by experts who have vetted them for accuracy. When collaborating with educators, provide examples of databases. Then learners can use those databases and compare that information with materials found on the Internet and in the news. Using databases is a worthwhile skill that can help learners identify reliable information. Research guides tailored to assignments and provided to learners are another way to encourage learners to take advantage of multiple sources.

Learners gather information appropriate to the task by collecting information representing diverse perspectives (Learner IV.B.2.). As different political and social groups attempt to assert that they are purveyors of "the Truth," it becomes beneficial for learners to collect information on current events, politics, and anything controversial from diverse perspectives (De Abreu 2021). The Media Bias Chart from adfontesmedia.com can help identify opposing viewpoints, as can some databases and websites. For the print collection and other curated resources that you provide learners, focus specifically on collecting viewpoints from marginalized groups.

The We Need Diverse Books website is a terrific place to diversify print collections. Becoming familiar with and exploring online communities from marginalized groups can yield terrific resources from other perspectives. People with disabilities, people embracing various religions, cultural and ethnic minority groups, LGBTQIA+ individuals, immigrant communities, and people embracing a range of political perspectives all deserve a voice in the resources that learners can access. Be careful not to fall into the trap we have heard often: "My school is not that diverse, so we don't need a diverse collection." This mindset leads to learners from homogenous communities growing up not understanding others and their differences. All learners need and deserve access to diverse perspectives.

In addition, consider curating translated books that were written outside the United States. Many times, when we think of diversity, we focus on Americanized viewpoints (Van Drie and Day 2023). Curating books that are from outside the United States enables students to learn from the global society through authentic viewpoints. Learners who are emergent bilinguals will appreciate books from their countries, and native English speakers will enjoy learning about other cultures. Look for books that have been translated to allow learners to compare texts in their native languages and English. The Global Literature in Libraries Initiative frequently updates the lists on its website.

As you curate materials to introduce diverse viewpoints, consider how you will help learners apply those viewpoints. One way to help learners communicate diverse viewpoints is to collaborate with other educators to create debate events. These events can help students learn how to access multiple sources of information to understand and validate divergent viewpoints. Furthermore, learners can produce their own resources, such as videos, presentations, infographics, and more, to validate the information sources by researching the viewpoints related to the debate topics.

Learners gather information appropriate to the task by systematically questioning and assessing the validity and accuracy of information (Learner IV.B.3.). Provide and teach frameworks for assessing sources. Consistently considering currency, accuracy, authority, purpose, bias, motivation, and other factors provides insight into the validity and accuracy of a piece of information. Work with learners and other educators to question sources to determine their usefulness based on validity and accuracy. Ensure that frameworks are understood and adopted by educators by providing ongoing professional development and integration across grade levels and subject areas. This work helps learners focus on applying the frameworks instead of adapting to each educator's specific preferences. Authority is contextual, and school librarians must move themselves and other educators away from the "because I said so" mindset to develop critical thinkers. A primary responsibility as educators is to teach learners how to learn, and the critical thinking required to question and assess the validity of information is a central component of lifelong learning (Lance and Maniotes 2020). Endeavor to create opportunities and an atmosphere that encourage learners to evaluate the information they discover and provide.

School librarians can collaborate with other educators to encourage learners to question sources by introducing a framework for questioning sources. Examples include Guided Inquiry (Kuhlthau, Maniotes, and Caspari 2015), the RADAR Framework (Mandalios 2013), and the SIFT process (Caulfield 2017). Lance and Maniotes (2020) have suggested implementing a whole-school effort in which school librarians first offer professional development so that educators can understand and adopt the frameworks for assignments. Learners are then exposed to these processes throughout the curriculum. School librarians can engage learners by offering support for their projects. This support is essential because "librarians who reported helping students with inquiry-based projects at least once a week said that their school and district leaders valued deeper learning, student questioning, critical thinking, global readiness, student engagement, application of learned content knowledge, and independent learning" (Lance and Maniotes 2020).

Learners gather information appropriate to the task by organizing information by priority, topic, or other systematic scheme (Learner IV.B.4.). Teach schemata for the organization of information so that it is accessible, shareable, and valuable. A straightforward example of teaching a schema involves practical lessons for learners, other educators, and administrators about organizing Google Drive folders. Teach how to devise a naming convention, such as numbering folders, so items appear in a predictable order in their drives. Examples include 1. Projects, 2. Assignments, and 3. Websites. In addition, demonstrate how to color-code Drive folders because colors are often recognized before names. Instruct learners to place every file in a folder and create subfolders to further classify files in their drives. Teach all learners to label their files with a descriptive name that may include a subject, date, and classroom educator's name. Finally, pair these lessons with tutorials for advanced search techniques in Google Drive that help learners find their files more efficiently.

The drop-down arrow to the right of the search box in Google Drive offers access to advanced search options. Learners can select the type of file they are looking for, along with its owner, location, and the date it was last modified. To make this search more efficient, include the item name. Remember, a file naming convention should be consistent. Alternatively, keywords from the file, such as a memorable line or the classroom educator's name, lesson, or unit, are helpful. Adding to the efficiency of Google Drive, learners can also search by file type (doc, sheet, slide, form, or drawing).

FIELD NOTE **Teaching Organization Schemes**

When working with young children, we must provide them with an organizing tool. The tool doesn't need to be complicated. My kids are still at the stage where comprehension and the relevance of what they are learning are instructional priorities. I focus on them organizing information. They are at the meaning-making level. So when we gather information, I provide them with the organization tool.

Last year, we went step by step through planning a research project. I modeled and guided practice on setting up an organizational system for research. First, we generated questions using background knowledge and what they wanted to know. They formed meaningful questions based on their interests.

It can be as simple as, "You've got four questions. Let's take this piece of paper and fold it in half twice. Now you have four boxes. Let's put one question in each box." Now, as we read about the research topic, learners can ask themselves:

1. Does the information I'm reading make sense to me?
2. Is the information meaningful to me?
3. Is it answering the questions I have about this topic?
4. Can I let this go, or do I need to hang on to this information?

Because they are so young and inexperienced with this kind of thinking, model this skill for them. Then further model how to take that new learning, summarize it, and synthesize it into the framework that we created together, recording their thoughts and learning.

This thinking process is *so* abstract for young readers that it needs to be addressed before tackling structure. I'd rather spend my time with young learners on meaning-making and provide them with a tool they can apply to many situations later in life. Once they have seen and used many organizational tools, they can later decide which would be best suited for a situation.

—Heather Picciuti (elementary school librarian, Texas)

Share

Learners exchange information resources within and beyond their learning community by accessing and evaluating collaboratively constructed information sites (Learner IV.C.1.). Wikipedia is an example of a collaboratively constructed information site. It is updated daily by more than 115,000 active editors (Wikipedia 2023). This site has high standards for content, requiring citations and links as well as reviews by other contributors. Examining community practices and articles about how Wikipedia came to be—and has survived and become one of the default sources of information for millions of people—might be a terrific project for social studies, language arts, or business classes. Challenges are associated with this potential activity because some educators still cling to the outdated belief that Wikipedia and other collaboratively constructed information sites are unreliable.

Leveraging learners' curiosity about a specific topic on a site such as Wikipedia is a perfect way to motivate them to evaluate the information they find on these sites. Teaching learners to evaluate these sources of information can focus on the inquiry and investigation skills that learners need to track down sources, rather than focusing on the container and its reputation. Here the process matters much more than the product, although the number of Wikipedia users shows how impactful a product can be.

Learners exchange information resources within and beyond their learning community by contributing to collaboratively constructed information sites by ethically using and reproducing others' work (Learner IV.C.2.). Familiar lessons on citing sources, including online citation builders, help learners build this Competency. Also consider the instruction provided about copyright, intellectual property, and accessing the remix culture for inspiration in remixing others' work. This Competency provides a space for school librarians to teach about Creative Commons and to license learners' creations for use by others. An important distinction here, missing from more traditional lessons, is that all learners, no matter their age, can be creators and be in control of how their work is published and built upon by others. Consider content created on video platforms and social media as well. Learners quickly point out that becoming a professional YouTuber is an actual job. This is an excellent opportunity to provide examples that help them understand how constantly getting takedown notifications for using others' copyrighted works can ruin a YouTuber's career.

Often, learners enjoy learning from each other. This Competency provides the opportunity for learners to become creators. Teaching learners to contribute to collaboratively constructed information sites can be done with familiar and easy-to-use tools. Along the way, share the Creative Commons licenses (figure 3.3; Creative Commons, n.d.) and attach them to learners' work. You can try these practical ideas right away:

- Teach learners how to create a Google Slides presentation collaboratively.
- Develop a Flip featuring book reviews.
- Create a class wiki or blog for learners to showcase and review the curation process of other learners.

While assisting learners with learning about the ethical use of others' work, you might review Google's CS First curriculum (2023). The curriculum is featured as part of the Libraries Ready to Code project (ALA, n.d.). Some lessons include remixing works created by others. The lessons are reinforced by the AASL Standards crosswalk with Google's CS First curriculum (AASL 2019a). The crosswalk will provide evidence about how using the lessons will support your school's curriculum.

Learners exchange information resources within and beyond their learning community by joining with others to compare and contrast information derived from collaboratively constructed information sites (Learner IV.C.3.). Crowdsourcing, triangulation, cross-checking, and fact-checking are all potential skills that learners can apply while building this Competency. Group projects are often the source of many groans from learners, and for a good reason. School librarians can influence how group projects unfold by creating opportunities for learners to become the group's fact-checker, triangulator, or corroboration expert, or many other roles that can prepare learners for working collaboratively and productively in a group to curate information from a variety of sources. Learning activities that release control to learners can create opportunities for learning within this Competency. For example, once a topic has been introduced in class, learners can be sent out to gather information on their own, then bring that information back to class or the group for evaluation, assessing currency, reliability, accuracy, and purpose as they go.

Choosing a Creative Commons license

STEP 1: CHOOSE LICENSE FEATURES

Publishing under a Creative Commons (CC) license is easy. First, choose the conditions that you want to apply to your work.

Attribution
All CC licenses require that others who use your work in any way must give you credit the way you request, but not in a way that suggests you endorse them or their use. If they want to use your work without giving you credit or for endorsement purposes, they must get your permission first.

ShareAlike
You let others copy, distribute, display, perform, and modify your work, as long as they distribute any modified work on the same terms. If they want to distribute modified works under other terms, they must get your permission first.

NoDerivs
You let others copy, distribute, display, and perform only original copies of your work. If they want to modify your work, they must get your permission first.

NonCommercial
You let others copy, distribute, display, perform, and (unless you have chosen NoDerivs) modify and use your work for any purpose other than commercially unless they get your permission first.

STEP 2: GET A LICENSE

Based on your choices, you will get a license that clearly indicates how other people may use your creative work.

Attribution
CC BY

Attribution—ShareAlike
CC BY-SA

Attribution—NoDerivs
CC BY-ND

Attribution—NonCommercial
CC BY-NC

Attribution—NonCommercial—ShareAlike
CC BY-NC-SA

Attribution—NonCommercial—NoDerivs
CC BY-NC-ND

Source: Creative Commons, n.d.

FIGURE 3.3 / **Choosing a Creative Commons license**

Grow

Learners select and organize information for a variety of audiences by performing ongoing analysis of and reflection on the quality, usefulness, and accuracy of curated resources (Learner IV.D.1.). School librarians can help learners develop this Competency by emphasizing quality over the speed at which assignments are completed and by working with other educators to ensure that learners are taught research and project skill sets. Educators frequently ask learners to research topics without teaching them how to accomplish the task. Spending class time in the research phase of projects is an excellent investment.

Assessing the quality of sources alongside the quality of student writing or creation is an important consideration here. For example, classroom educators can be advised to consider assessing the final product of a project as only 10 percent of the overall grade. The remaining 90 percent of the grade can reflect the process phase of project-based learning because the process is where the learning happens. Focusing the assessment on the final product reinforces the belief that the end justifies the means. The misconception that the learning process is less critical than the end product frequently leads to plagiarism. Learners rush through projects instead of reflecting on and learning from the research and creation processes. As a result, learners may develop a disdain for project-based learning.

Over time, learners (and educators) will understand that ongoing analysis and reflection are where the learning happens and that the finished learning product is simply icing on the cake. Learners become more critical, systematic, and reflective about the information they access and use, and isn't that what we want for our future leaders?

Learners select and organize information for a variety of audiences by integrating and depicting in a conceptual knowledge network their understanding gained from resources (Learner IV.D.2.). School librarians can influence learners' lives by modeling making connections with prior knowledge and asking learners to draw connections between their previous learning and what they are currently studying. School librarians are uniquely positioned to work with learners throughout their primary education years. Although learners may get new classroom educators as they change grade levels and courses each year, learners will probably have the same school librarian for several years.

Learners must be given opportunities to build connections between academic topics and personal areas of interest and between new knowledge and previous units of study (Hattan and Lupo 2020). It is helpful when every grade level and subject area creates connections between curated resources and their units of study. Library activities that reference curriculum areas and allow the exploration of personal interests make learning applicable to real-world situations. Learners understand how the lessons apply to them when they finish their formal education.

Learners need to depict their understanding of what they have learned from resources and share their understanding with their knowledge networks. Class discussion boards, blogs, and wikis allow learners to share their prior knowledge and the new knowledge that they have gained. Another low-tech way in which learners can connect and share information is to post K-W-L and KWHLAQ charts in the school library or in their classrooms. K-W-L and KWHLAQ charts answer the questions in table 3.4. The K-W-L chart is more suitable for primary grade levels (e.g., pre-kindergarten–second grade). Learners can share their understanding of new knowledge and the connection to prior knowledge during Round Robin and Think-Pair-Share activities.

TABLE 3.4 /

Questions for checking for understanding and connecting prior knowledge

K-W-L	KWHLAQ
K (What do I know?) W (What do I want to know?) L (What did I learn?)	K (What do I know?) W (What do I want to know?) H (How do I find out?) L (What did I learn?) A (What action can I take?) Q (What new questions do I have?)

Learners select and organize information for a variety of audiences by openly communicating curation processes for others to use, interpret, and validate (Learner IV.D.3.). When learners share their curation processes with each other, educators, and community members, learners increase their understanding of the work they do and of how the work they are doing in class and on personal projects helps them achieve their goals. As education continues to transform, this relationship between concepts previously taught and concepts learned in isolation potentially makes a difference for learners and helps them see their formal education as vital to their success. Curation skills cut across every subject area, unit of study, and informal learning on the playground and outside school. When learners can openly communicate their curation strategies and get feedback from others, they become empowered to apply those strategies in all areas of their lives.

Are you still wondering how you can help learners share their curation processes? It is not as hard as you may think. The following activities can provide meaningful experiences:

- Use peer-review rubrics in small groups.
- Host workshops in which learners can share their findings and provide feedback to others.
- Host a poster session in the school library to showcase exceptional projects.
- Invite learners to the morning show to discuss their research findings and how they arrived at them.
- Create templates that learners can fill in and compare to guide their inquiry processes.

Sparking Learners' Interest in Curation

We began this chapter by noting that school librarians have long been curating materials for learners. Our best practices are delineated in the *National School Library Standards*. Much of what the profession is recognized for is embedded in our collection-development skills. However, school librarians are educators first, and much of what we do relates to how we teach our learners to be effective curators to support their academic and personal interests.

Creating an environment to facilitate the development of competent curators requires school librarians to reach beyond the confines of the library walls and embrace collaborative relationships with learners, other educators, and our communities. The journey toward teaching Curate Competencies may also require a change in the pedagogy mindset. Specifically, teaching learners how to curate materials to articulate meaningful results necessitates committing to an emphasis on quality research that results in exceptional end products.

Learning the curation process should not be rushed. Allowing learners to savor the process of exploring content and using background knowledge promotes enjoyment in the research process instead of anxiety. And of course, along the way, we teach our learners how to organize their collections, fact-check, and identify quality materials. Indeed, school librarians can ignite the flame that sparks learners to become competent curators of personal collections.

Questions for the Reflective Practitioner

1. What changes can I make to collaborating with colleagues to better support learners as curators exploring their personal interests?
2. How can I determine learners' current aptitude and competency for collecting, organizing, and sharing relevant information?
3. What instructional strategies can I use to build interest and create relevancy for learners around curation activities?

4 Modeling Curate Competencies

What value do school librarians add to learners' journeys through instruction in curation? Though other responsibilities often take precedence, teaching is the primary role. School librarians create opportunities to teach because the library is often a flexible space, without the constraints of a specific curriculum or high-stakes tests. School librarians teach multiple literacy skills in collaboration with educator partners to ensure that learners develop the knowledge and skills needed to be successfully "prepared for college, career, and life" (AASL 2018, 12).

The *National School Library Standards* present a strong connection between school librarian roles (AASL 2018, 14–16) and how those roles relate to learners and school library activities. Figure 4.1 (on the following page) illustrates the connections between the roles of the school librarian, the Domains in the AASL Standards Frameworks, and learners.

Modeling the Domains within Our Roles

The Curate Shared Foundation provides a solid platform for leveraging school librarian roles to ensure services for learners, educator partners, and communities at a high level. As *leaders* within schools and districts, school librarians curate relationships with stakeholders that help librarians understand and effectively act upon community challenges and opportunities. The *instructional partner* role emphasizes collaborating with other educators and the community to solve instructional challenges using thoughtfully curated resources, experiences, and relationships to enhance the delivery of instruction for learners. Chapter 5 discusses instruction in the school library, and examples of activities are provided in the appendix, "Curation Lesson Starters."

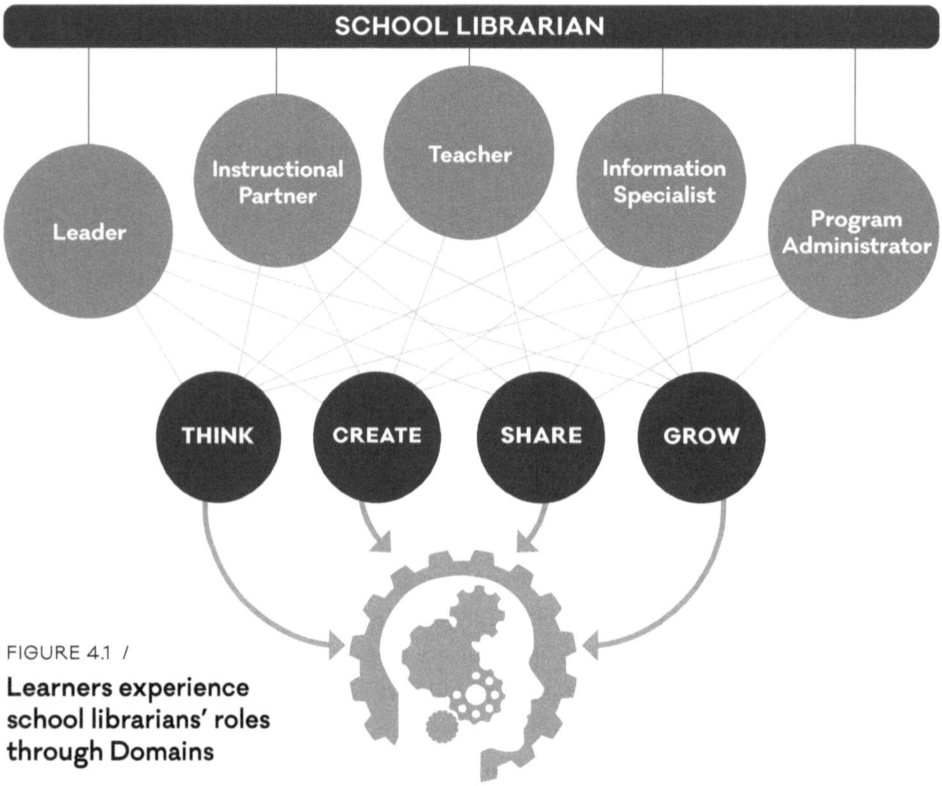

FIGURE 4.1 /
Learners experience school librarians' roles through Domains

The *information specialist* role is closely connected with the Curate Shared Foundation in that resources, practices, policies, and connections are continually curated to improve instruction. School librarians represent schools and districts locally and globally to lead the vital work of reimagining what school can be for learners and communities. As *program administrators*, school librarians ensure equitable access to libraries and curated physical and virtual resources.

Finally, the *teacher* role within the Domains creates space and opportunity for curation work to take center stage. School librarians empower learners and educators to become "critical thinkers, enthusiastic readers, skillful researchers, and ethical users of information" (AASL 2009, 18). Although the Curate Shared Foundation connects deeply with all the preceding roles, it is in the instructional role that curated resources play the most significant part. After all, how can teaching be effective without these resources? Curation must occur before learners, and other educators, can be provided opportunities to Think, Create, Share, and Grow.

Coaching Critical Curators through the Domains

Aligning the Curate Shared Foundation with the various curricula in schools and providing professional development for other educators will yield the best opportunities for teaching others to curate for themselves. In this chapter, school librarian Competencies are shared, with examples of curation instruction for learners and other educators.

Think

School librarians challenge learners to act on an information need by modeling the response to a need to gather and organize information (School Librarian IV.A.1.). School librarians model this response to an information need by sharing collection-development strategies and tools. Examples include openly exploring collection-development policies and procedures during learning community discussions, creating accounts in book purchasing software for learner and educator recommendations, and giving school library users a voice in collection development. School librarians must express why they put so much time and effort into organizing our school libraries—why the books are arranged as they are, and why it is necessary to make online information accessible. This instruction can be woven into orientation sessions and collaborative instruction. When school librarians model the need for information organization, learners are connected to the concept of curating for others' access versus collecting for self-interests.

When teaching learners, model the behaviors you wish to see in them as you model learning strategies and tools. Show them how to apply strategies to locate, access, evaluate, and use information for specific needs. When presenting research strategies, consider narrating your thought process as you search, describing why you use specific keywords. Teach learners to practice lateral reading. *Lateral reading* is the process of verifying the information that is being read (Stanford History Education Group, n.d.). For instance, if a learner finds a statistic in an article, they can verify whether that statistic is correct by consulting another information source. Individuals practicing lateral reading may skim two texts to determine the credibility of the information that needs to be verified. Lateral reading works well with skimming techniques. However, these concepts are foreign to learners if they are not modeled. Help your learners understand how you have developed habits and routines—such as creating citations, saving articles, and preserving other media—and how these works are connected to fill an information need. Although structured classes and professional development events are efficient for teaching these skills, teachable moments may emerge during small-group discussions, after-school enrichment activities, and reference interviews.

Take modeling these strategies a step further by encouraging active learning. As learners reflect on the behaviors you are displaying, ask learners to mimic those behaviors. Then learners can practice and verbalize the strategies in their curation work. Please encourage learners to discuss their thought processes or share those processes during group work. It is effective to ask learners to sketch out their ideas for later assessment by you or in collaboration with a classroom educator. In addition, consistently sharing the *why* behind specific collection-development strategies and tools helps learners and other educators understand how the school library collection addresses community needs.

School librarians challenge learners to act on an information need by designing opportunities for learners to explore possible information sources (School Librarian IV.A.2.). Opportunities to design curation activities are often developed in collaboration with other educators to support assignments and projects. Although school librarians help learners explore extracurricular and personal interests, curation opportunities are less likely to be developed in isolation, especially at the secondary level. Learners will not likely access and use school library resources independently unless they have a compelling personal need for information. It is more likely for learners to discover curated collections when a classroom educator uses the school library for a unit or lesson.

Creating opportunities for collaboration with classroom educators while accommodating busy schedules is an enormous challenge (Merga et al., 2021). Although collaborative instruction is ideal, collaboration is often harder in elementary school settings, where library time is often a part of the specials rotation. However, offering learning assessments can open doors for reluctant educators. When opportunities arise, school librarians can offer to provide a pre-assessment and to co-plan, co-teach, *and* co-assess collaborative lessons, units, or projects. School librarians can work with learners to build background knowledge using curated resources and can provide project or group work time, space, and curated resources for assignments. At the elementary level, the school librarian can offer a portion of the library rotation schedule to conduct enrichment activities for an existing unit.

It is possible to draw learners into curated collections through programming and creative orientations, such as escape or breakout units, and through curating engaging spaces, materials, or experiences. For instance, you could circulate makerspace kits (bit.ly/ETLSMakers). Through makerspace kits, school librarians and their educator partners can authentically engage learners by making available learning tools that are outside the usual paper/pencil/laptop experiences. Robots, building sets, 3-D printing, and other hands-on experiences are indeed information sources. They allow learners to interact with information rather than consume it.

School librarians challenge learners to act on an information need by guiding learners to make critical choices about information sources to use (School Librarian IV.A.3.). Emphasize quality over speed. Educators generally are not interested in how quickly learners find information. They care about the quality of the information that learners find and use. It is advantageous for learners to interact with experts in the field, such as journalists, bloggers, and hobbyists. One of the significant innovations in technology and the Internet is that everyone has a voice. One critical skill that learners should use regularly is determining which voices move a conversation forward, which voices lend a unique perspective on a subject, and which voices add no value to the conversation.

Teaching this skill is complex—it takes time to help learners understand how to critique their sources and to guide them in analyzing information sources and in determining their origins and the motivations for creating them. One strategy for imparting this skill is to teach lateral reading whereby learners conduct research on someone who has created a potentially beneficial piece of information. In a digital environment, research often involves opening a new browser tab and searching for the person, along with keywords such as "credentials," "background," or even "criticism."

Practical Applications of Curate/Think

- Teach learners the SIFT framework and lateral reading.
- Create research guides for learners based on the curriculum.
- Model data literacy skills by displaying school library statistics, conducting surveys or focus groups, and sharing results.
- Feature the results of collaborative co-teaching projects in the school library and on the library website.
- Align library lessons with the scope and sequence of the curriculum, and implement the lessons at least one week before the classroom educators begin a unit. Then, advertise the library lesson sequence.

Create

School librarians promote information gathering appropriate to the task by sharing a variety of sources (School Librarian IV.B.1.). School librarians must move beyond print and traditional library databases to open educational resources (OERs) and other expert-curated resources. This step will enable the sharing of a plethora of sources with other educators and learners. Hashtags, videos, and other community resources also have value. Incorporating these resources into learners' work when collaborating with other educators can broaden educators' and learners' perspectives of "acceptable" source material. Redefine primary sources for your school community to be more inclusive. Refinement includes presenting historically marginalized perspectives, lived experiences, oral histories, college and university repositories, open-source academic journals, and other authentic voices in your curated collections.

Part of including diverse voices and experiences is remembering that curation cannot happen in a vacuum, with school librarians sitting in offices or behind circulation desks making lists of books to buy.

> Clearly, there's a need to curate media of all types. School librarians no longer need to worry about storing content by format. While materials may continue to be siloed by vendor or publishers' names, librarians now have the ability to pull together virtual shelves that are format and device agnostic. (Valenza and Stephens 2015)

Our curation responsibilities include creating virtual repositories for resources and tools in all formats, whereby we organize, describe, and make accessible an array of resources for our school communities.

Besides creating repositories, expose learners to different tools to describe and organize media. Exposing learners to new tools can begin with a curated list that describes the purpose of the tools. Carefully incorporate the tools into projects. It is always helpful to provide examples of how tools can be used. Either create these examples or link the tools to examples and tutorials.

Another way to expose learners to new tools is to align the tools with curricular activities and offer workshops to educators to teach them about the tools (Smith et al., 2022). Educators who have concrete examples of how tools can be used in the classroom, along with ongoing support, are more likely to choose new digital tools over traditional teaching methods. Moreover, arranging for other educators and learners who have been successful in using digital tools to showcase their results will encourage more people to adopt the tools (Smith et al., 2022).

Involvement in a robust professional learning community and being active in professional organizations expose school librarians to new resources. No single human being can overcome the pace of innovation in educational technology. New apps, websites, and digital tools are introduced, upgraded, bought, merged, or shut down daily. As school librarians curate tools to organize and describe media, learners are best served by focusing our efforts on tools that satisfy selection requirements. Specifically, curate tools and your sources. School librarians should also model the mindsets that learners and other educators must develop to shift from one tool to another seamlessly. Change is hard. Try to clarify how tools are similar, the advantages of changing tools, and when to switch tools when organizing and describing media.

School librarians promote information gathering appropriate to the task by encouraging the use of information representing diverse perspectives (School Librarian IV.B.2.). Libraries of all types have focused on authority as a basic standard by which we describe, select, promote, and teach who the experts in a field might be. Part of that established practice has perpetuated ugly, racist practices in librarianship (Sierpe 2019). Curating underrepresented and minority voices, unpopular views, challenging perspectives, and voices outside the mainstream can assist with undoing some of the damage and trauma that librarianship has inflicted upon society.

Consider curating eyewitness accounts of events alongside media accounts. Carefully selected zines and other media can be timely and representative of the learners' and community's backgrounds (Ehlers 2020). Strive to represent voices that reflect diversity in, but are not limited to, race, religion, ethnicity, and socioeconomic levels. Share perspectives from around the world, especially countries represented in learner populations. Learners in schools that do not have diverse populations must be exposed to multicultural concepts and be taught from diverse materials. Exposure to multicultural viewpoints builds empathy. When learners, educators, and communities do not see and acknowledge others' lived experiences, those experiences become easier to dismiss if confronted with their effects.

Once you have curated resources representing diverse viewpoints, consider marketing the materials. Create eye-catching book displays, bulletin boards, and digital flyers that can be posted to social media. Recruit members of the school community to share their favorite picks and why those resources are their favorites. Contests that feature the materials will also promote curiosity and encourage learners to access them.

School librarians promote information gathering appropriate to the task by fostering the questioning and assessing of validity and accuracy of information (School Librarian IV.B.3.). Teaching research strategies such as triangulation, multiple source verification, lateral reading, and questioning of creators' motivations and biases helps develop this Competency in learners. Learners should understand

Practical Applications of Curate/Create

- Host a hackathon to solve a community problem.
- Provide copies of your school library policies for collection development and discuss them with your school community.
- Show examples of ways to organize information, including graphic organizers, charts, reference lists, and file naming conventions and arrangements.
- Host a school news show that allows learners to interview school community members about their opinions on important topics.
- Create a resource folder with subfolders in Google Drive, and use it as an example when showing learners how to organize their files.

and be able to discuss the inherent differences between and advantages of using materials from databases, books, news outlets, and bloggers. For example, a well-established news outlet that features trained journalists may have more-creditable information than will a random blogger. Vetted books from creditable publishers and databases have an advantage over websites produced by predatory companies that seek to provide subjective viewpoints (Pilgrim et al., 2019). Assessing learners for these skills works with collaborative instruction with other educators. Share the processes used for curation, and invite learners to question sources, such as print and database resources, that have been seen as authoritative with little critical consideration.

School librarians promote information gathering appropriate to the task by providing tools and strategies to organize information by priority, topic, or other systematic scheme (School Librarian IV.B.4.). School librarians model and teach the importance of considering different perspectives to investigate topics. Learners need to understand how to keep track of their sources by creating citations, works cited pages, and a repository of links as they work. Cross-checking resources will result in the collection of several resources that need to be documented.

Similarly, as school librarians teach learners and other educators to use tools to organize information, teaching about metadata also becomes essential. Learners can use tagging related to subject headings, source types, author's reputation, and other criteria to organize their content. Try to instill in the school community the importance of keeping Google Drive folders and files highly organized by sharing how the resources can easily be accessed each school year. Demonstrate that every file and folder can have a descriptive filename, that folders can be color-coded, and that subfolders may organize related materials together. Well-organized materials can ease anxiety among learners and new educators.

Organization techniques are beneficial because they enable the quick and efficient location of resources. Advanced learners can be taught to hyperlink their Google Drive resources by creating hyperdocs. Accessing one hyperdoc can reveal all related resources. Such organizing soon becomes a habit, encouraging educators and learners to develop an appreciation for the work of systematically arranging and describing resources.

Share

School librarians contribute to and guide information resource exchange within and beyond the school learning community by facilitating opportunities to access and evaluate collaboratively constructed information sites (School Librarian IV.C.1.). Many schools, especially high schools and colleges, have hosted edit-a-thons for Wikipedia or other sites. These events expose learners to the writing, verification, and editing processes. Edited works are posted on a resource like Wikipedia. These experiences provide opportunities for learners to practice evaluation skills and add their knowledge to one of the world's most consulted sources of information. Moreover, learners see how resources like Wikipedia came to be and gain a better understanding of the editorial process and the rigorous evaluation needed to create these resources.

Learner-created class websites with similar evaluation methods can also be developed and devoted to a topic, project, or unit of study. The term *information sites* can be expanded to include any learning product collaboratively constructed, including, but not limited to, video, audio, multimedia, virtual reality, and other products that invite the integration of information and skills gained from various sources. As these learning products are integrated into instruction, teaching learners to evaluate works themselves offers a tremendous benefit. Learners will become accustomed to thinking critically about the resources they are accessing.

School librarians contribute to and guide information resource exchange within and beyond the school learning community by devising pathways for learners to contribute to collaboratively constructed information sites by ethically using and reproducing others' work (School Librarian IV.C.2.). In addition to the familiar research paper or project, learners could work with the community in creating and digitizing local history resources, cooperating with genealogists and historical societies, the public library, and other entities. Such projects provide practice in reading, analyzing, and synthesizing historical documents, connecting learners to the history of the area in which they live and providing context as they explore why their community has developed as it has. As learners engage in real-world applications that require using and remixing others' work, learners are exposed to numerous instances in which they must apply information ethics.

Regardless of the projects the school library supports, school librarians can help learners achieve quality results in elementary school, middle school, high school, and beyond. For example, school librarians can teach learners how to preserve their work after graduation. School librarians can work with educator partners to assist learners in developing portfolios, online repositories, or websites tied to learners' district accounts as backups. During these efforts, consider the mobility of the learner population. Teach other educators and learners the importance of file structures and naming conventions in folder-based applications like Google Drive or Microsoft 365. Color-coding, subfolders, and naming files for searchability will assist learners in quickly locating what they need. Teach these skills directly to learners and in professional development sessions.

FIELD NOTE

Teaching Learners How to Use Databases for Curation

When I go into classrooms to help learners find sources in the Gale database, I teach them how to color-code the subtopics they are searching. Then I introduce them to the tools within Gale. I show them how to highlight information within an article and color-code it to match their subtopics. Then they make notes using the "notecards" found in the tools and record the citation. When they are done, learners can send the article straight to their OneDrive, where the article appears with the highlights, notes, and citations for when they return later.

—Lesleigh Lynes (high school library media specialist, Oklahoma)

School librarians contribute to and guide information resource exchange within and beyond the school learning community by directing learners to join others to compare and contrast information derived from collaboratively constructed information sites (School Librarian IV.C.3.). School librarians are well positioned to facilitate learners' work with community members. Enthusiasts, experts, and learners of all ages value and should be presented with opportunities to share their knowledge and understanding with others. For instance, community members can offer tutoring, give expert opinions for assignments, and be presenters for interactive library programming. Programming that connects the community to the school through the school library is an excellent prospect for instructing learners in the hard skills of comparing and contrasting information and the soft skills of collaboration and teamwork.

Learners can see the soft skills of effective collaboration in action as they watch school librarians interact with community members. Conversely, to serve as role models, school librarians need to be open and honest about successful and unsuccessful collaboration experiences with others. One type of project that evidences this Competency is the often maligned group assignment. School librarians can make these experiences more palatable by helping other educators focus on and assess the learning process and learning products. If the value is placed on learners' ability to compare and contrast information rather than on the information they obtain from collaboratively constructed information sites, then the assessment of their work matters. Traditionally, learners might be assessed on how many sources they find. With the school librarian's help, classroom educators can place more emphasis on quality rather than quantity by collaboratively developing a rubric, or adopting one of the many available online, for assessing and evaluating the information found on these sites. Helping learners compare and contrast their work can be as simple as using graphic organizers or prompting them to verbally share the information they have found and writing the differences in their content and approaches to finding information. Comparing and contrasting the information found is only one portion of this work, and they are critical steps in triangulation, cross-checking, and verification—all vital to ensuring that our learners are accessing and using the best information available in their work.

Practical Applications of Curate/Share

- Teach learners how to design blogs and wikis that include reference lists.
- Explain Creative Commons licenses to learners and then collaborate with other educators to design a lesson about creating resources that can be remixed.
- Start a Wakelet or Padlet for educators and learners to share their favorite curriculum resources.
- Start a coding club that uses lessons from Libraries Ready to Code and explain how coders often share code and give credit for the code they use.
- Collaborate with the public library to supplement the collection and design summer or after-school programming.

Grow

School librarians show learners how to select and organize information for a variety of audiences by engaging learners in ongoing analysis of and reflection on the quality, usefulness, and accuracy of curated resources (School Librarian IV.D.1.). An effective strategy for guiding learners through analysis and reflective activities relating to curated sources is to conduct a think-aloud. This activity can be done in all instructional settings—with entire classes, small groups, and one-to-one interaction. School librarians can collaborate with another educator to review assignments from a learner perspective, breaking down the prompts and requirements in real time and explaining the thinking process. The other educator's objectives and expectations for learners assist the school librarian in progressing through an assignment from the learner's perspective, applying their knowledge, experience, and expertise. The activity is particularly helpful when collaborating with the other educator in advance to learn about the features of an ideal response to an assignment.

A common shortcoming of many assignments is the lack of opportunity for learners to deeply analyze or reflect on how a topic, controversy, conflict, or event truly affected themselves and our society. School librarians should help incorporate high-level analysis and reflection into the class assignments created and revised with educator partners when planning lessons and units. Practical opportunities can include sharing reflections on assignments through presentations, discussions with guest presenters from the community, and collaborative sites such as Padlet or Google Jamboard.

School librarians can address inequity by thoughtfully and intentionally curating, and exposing other educators and learners to, lesser-known but equally meaningful resources from outside the mainstream publishing community (Van Drie and Day 2023). These sources can come from searching X (formerly known as Twitter) hashtags that address specific social issues, such as #immigration and #racism. Another strategy is to read extensively in the areas of study covered in your school's curriculum that have been glossed over by social studies textbooks. Partner with other educators to do deeper dives into topics that do not involve wars and political leaders, as history, to use one example, often does.

School librarians show learners how to select and organize information for a variety of audiences by formulating tasks that help learners to integrate and depict in a conceptual knowledge network learners' understanding gained from resources (School Librarian IV.D.2.). Developing a robust conceptual knowledge network requires school librarians and learners to read widely and deeply in various areas, both for academic pursuits and to satisfy their intellectual curiosity. No one in a school is better positioned to help learners connect knowledge gained from various grade levels and subject areas than the school librarian, who serves learners throughout their entire time at a school, not just during a single academic year (Litvinov 2023). Building a robust conceptual knowledge network is one of the fundamental purposes of education because this work sets learners up for success both in school and later in life. The more learners know, the easier it becomes for them to integrate new knowledge into their existing knowledge network.

Consider a musician who understands music theory and can read musical notation. It would be much easier for this person to pick up an unfamiliar instrument and play it than for someone who has never studied music or played *any* instrument before. The musician's conceptual knowledge network in music theory, composition, and performance is far more developed than that of someone who has never extensively studied or played music.

The same can be said for learners (and adults) who read voraciously and widely. They have been exposed to far more ideas, writing styles, vocabulary, themes, and subjects than has someone who reads casually, in a single genre, or not at all. It is far more efficient for voracious readers to add to their conceptual knowledge networks. Making connections between new knowledge and their existing experiences requires far less effort than it would for someone who is not widely read. Remember that "reading" here also encompasses media formats other than text, such as audio and video. Virtual formats also count as "reading" because our brains must decode and then similarly encode information.

Now that we have discussed conceptual knowledge networks, let's think about collaborating with classroom educators to create or modify learning tasks to strengthen those networks. Collaboration can generate projects that help learners understand how resources relate to their personal experiences and the real world. Being able to articulate these connections inspires learners. Depicting connections between resources also lends to a more significant study for learners and an understanding of the processes involved in resource analysis and evaluation.

Examples of these depictions include creative projects such as podcasts, posters (both digital and physical), sketchnotes, design thinking projects to solve problems, K-W-L charts, or short essays. Choose multiple forms of depictions to allow learners to express themselves in a conformable medium. Start with a prompt such as "Before this project, I knew ____. On the basis of my research, I know ____." Articulations of connections assist learners in arriving at the "right" answer and gaining a deep understanding of and appreciation for the context in which that information exists.

School librarians show learners how to select and organize information for a variety of audiences by making opportunities for learners to openly communicate curation processes for others to use, interpret, and validate (School Librarian IV.D.3.). Encouraging peer review of curation activities and processes represents a potentially significant and disruptive shift from traditional education, in which learners have been expected to communicate and share their understanding of a single subject or objective solely with the educator assessing their work. Bringing other learners into the curation process creates opportunities for deeper engagement in, thought about, and valuing of the learning process than does the more traditional emphasis on the learning product. Educators can create structures for learners to share their curation work with others. Peer review prepares learners to seek, accept, and incorporate peer feedback into the research and decision-making processes. These skills represent the growth mindset typically needed in collaborative work environments.

School librarians must be at the forefront of connecting our schools, educators, and learners to the outside world. Making these connections fulfills the purpose of school librarians in several ways, mainly that of providing opportunities for learners to practice and share their own curation processes and products with others. Building upon learner interaction, school librarians can create opportunities for open communication about the curation process by providing access to and instruction on curation tools, strategies, and understanding of discoverability, organization, and sharing of curated information and resources. School librarians should always search for opportunities to leverage learners' passions and apply the Competencies of the Curate Shared Foundation to learners' daily, nonacademic lives.

Practical Applications of Curate/Grow

- Create opportunities for learners to engage in peer assessment and to reflect on how information is gathered for projects.
- Collaborate with educators to support and facilitate debates about curricular topics.
- Teach lessons that show how learners can discuss divergent viewpoints cordially. Include examples of questions that learners can ask to assess the quality of information shared during the discussion.
- Analyze state data from standardized tests and data about the collections of similar libraries to make data-based decisions about your collection and programming.
- Solicit learner help with creating book and resource reviews for the school library. Use a system to rate the qualities of the books and resources.

School Librarians as Curation Role Models

Perhaps this chapter can be eloquently summarized by stating that school librarians are curation role models. Our efforts in showing learners how to implement curation processes make a difference in how their skills manifest for academic achievement. After all, we can point to numerous studies showing that school librarians are linked to academic achievement. Don't feel pressured, though. We can leverage the Curate Shared Foundation to empower learners to invest in their education by thinking critically to become ethical curators of information.

We have shared several practical applications to serve as guides for initiating activities or boosting the programming that you already provide. As you implement our suggestions, encourage learners to continuously communicate about their curation processes by discussing your own. Reflective practice and assessment of the quality, intent, and accuracy of resources will reinforce your learners' ability to build their conceptual knowledge networks and independent curation behaviors.

Questions for the Reflective Practitioner

1. Which Domains do I currently model well in my curation instruction? Which Domains or specific school librarian Competencies have I identified as needing improvement?
2. How can modeling the Curate Shared Foundation with learners and other educators help me cultivate a culture of curators within my learning community?
3. Who is a potential partner that can help me "level up" my curation instruction? What aspects of curation may appeal to this partner and why?

5

Developing Lifelong Curators

School librarians innovating instruction aligned with the Curate Shared Foundation can immediately affect learners and other educators by teaching inquiry skills. For example, instead of pulling books from the school library collection to create a cart for a unit, collaborate with classroom educators to maximize the library experience. Most educators want a competent partner who can enhance their instructional efforts. Teach educators and learners to conduct advanced searches in the online public access catalog (OPAC) to find books. "Learners must identify all possible sources of information: traditional print resources as well as digital formats" (AASL 2018, 96). Teach them to access and use databases, curated resources, and OERs. Curation instruction that teaches inquiry skills accomplishes several objectives:

- Educators and learners take control of their teaching and learning by curating for themselves.
- School librarians expose educators and learners to the vast array of choices available in the library collection while providing tools and strategies for making choices manageable.
- Educators and learners become more likely to turn to school librarian–curated resources to meet their next information need because they understand there is a difference between random items about a topic and carefully selected materials.
- School librarians can build upon the newfound knowledge of educators and learners to enable curation instruction at higher levels, using a more comprehensive array of resources.

Scaffolding is a vital concept in teaching and learning that can help educators and learners develop curation competencies. Scaffolding breaks instruction into small lessons and provides instructional support to assist with learning skills (Puntambekar 2022). Significant scaffolding must be used for younger learners and learners inexperienced with curation. “Because learners do not master a competency in a single day or through a single activity, measure growth along the way to evaluate progress” (AASL 2018, 133).

However, many educators miss the key concept that scaffolds are temporary and are to be taken down once learners exhibit an acceptable level of competence. For example, in a thoughtfully articulated elementary school library program, significant time is dedicated to explicit instruction in curation tools in the early grades and at the beginning of each school year for all grades. As learners become more familiar with the school library and its collections, school librarians can remove the scaffolds of explicit instruction and progress to nuanced conversations about specific books, authors, or online tools that learners can access and use. School librarians often begin by using print materials with their youngest learners and prepare them for finding appropriate books by curating the easiest-to-read books into special school library sections or bins.

School librarians should share the scaffolds they are using and their purpose during instruction. Otherwise, scaffolds may interfere with learners’ experiences outside school libraries. A school librarian may explain to learners that academic and public libraries are not genrefied. For example, the school librarian should explain to elementary learners that animal books are not likely to be found in a special blue bin. Instead, the books can be discovered by using OPACs, locating the 500s section in the library, or engaging with online resources such as databases.

Sharing these details with learners will enable them to become independent resource explorers. In the future, exploring the library and its virtual and print materials and the organizational structures within those materials will make information accessible to learners for the rest of their lives. Library lessons that encourage learners to search for readily available resources through scaffolding will strengthen their information literacy skills.

School librarians must embed curation skills and tools into the curriculum and align instruction with the Domains and Competencies of the Curate Shared Foundation. Although school librarians should have a general understanding of the school curriculum, it is impossible to be an expert in all subject areas. The curation skills necessary for each subject are complex, layered, and specific to each learning community or instructional opportunity. Therefore, a holistic view of needed skills can be gained only through collaborating with other educators to create learning activities for content areas, units, and lessons.

Aligning Standards to Create Opportunity

School librarians can identify opportunities for collaboratively teaching curation by observing other educators or asking about their day-to-day classroom instruction, projects, research assignments, and extended units of study. Tables 5.1 and 5.2 (on the following pages) provide the foundation for an alignment between the *AASL Standards Framework for Learners* and the Common Core State Standards (CCSS) using one Learner Competency from each of the four Domains within the Curate Shared Foundation. The tables show one English language arts (ELA) standard from the Common Core for each grade level.

As you review these alignments, consider new ideas for lessons and what you may already be doing with your learners that supports the alignment. Note that the charts are rudimentary and that more alignments exist. Although every state has not adopted the CCSS, the standards outline the foundational skills used to assess learners. For this book, the standards have been used to provide just one example and a beginning to integrating curation instruction.

TABLE 5.1 / **AASL Standards sample alignment with Common Core State Standards (kindergarten–sixth grade)**

Shared Foundation IV. Curate

AASL Standards Framework for Learners	COMMON CORE STATE STANDARDS English Language Arts Standards		
	K	**1**	**2**
THINK **IV.A.1.** Learners act on an information need by determining the need to gather information.	**CCSS.ELA-LITERACY.RI.K.1:** With prompting and support, ask and answer questions about key details in a text.	**CCSS.ELA-LITERACY.W.1.2:** Write informative/explanatory texts in which they name a topic, supply some facts about the topic, and provide some sense of closure.	**CCSS.ELA-LITERACY.W.2.7:** Participate in shared research and writing projects (e.g., read a number of books on a single topic to produce a report; record science observations).
CREATE **IV.B.2.** Learners gather information appropriate to the task by collecting information representing diverse perspectives.	**CCSS.ELA-LITERACY.RI.K.7:** With prompting and support, describe the relationship between illustrations and the text in which they appear (e.g., what person, place, thing, or idea in the text an illustration depicts).	**CCSS.ELA-LITERACY.RI.1.9:** Identify basic similarities in and differences between two texts on the same topic (e.g., in illustrations, descriptions, or procedures).	**CCSS.ELA-LITERACY.RI.2.9:** Compare and contrast the most important points presented by two texts on the same topic.
SHARE **IV.C.2.** Learners exchange information resources within and beyond their learning community by contributing to collaboratively constructed information sites by ethically using and reproducing others' work.	**CCSS.ELA-LITERACY.W.K.7:** Participate in shared research and writing projects (e.g., explore a number of books by a favorite author and express opinions about them).	**CCSS.ELA-LITERACY.W.1.7:** Participate in shared research and writing projects (e.g., explore a number of "how-to" books on a given topic and use them to write a sequence of instructions).	**CCSS.ELA-LITERACY.W.2.7:** Participate in shared research and writing projects (e.g., read a number of books on a single topic to produce a report; record science observations).
GROW **IV.D.1.** Learners select and organize information for a variety of audiences by performing ongoing analysis of and reflection on the quality, usefulness, and accuracy of curated resources.	**CCSS.ELA-LITERACY.RI.K.6:** Name the author and illustrator of a text and define the role of each in presenting the ideas or information in a text.	**CCSS.ELA-LITERACY.RI.1.6:** Distinguish between information provided by pictures or other illustrations and information provided by the words in a text.	**CCSS.ELA-LITERACY.RI.2.6:** Identify the main purpose of a text, including what the author wants to answer, explain, or describe.

Source: CCSS alignment created by Len Bryan for Denver (Colorado) Public Schools.

KEY COMMITMENT: Make meaning for oneself and others by collecting, organizing, and sharing resources of personal relevance.

COMMON CORE STATE STANDARDS English Language Arts Standards			
3	**4**	**5**	**6**
CCSS.ELA-LITERACY.W.3.7: Conduct short research projects that build knowledge about a topic.	**CCSS.ELA-LITERACY. W.4.2.B:** Develop the topic with facts, definitions, concrete details, quotations, or other information and examples related to the topic.	**CCSS.ELA-LITERACY. W.5.2.A:** Introduce a topic clearly, provide a general observation and focus, and group related information logically; include formatting (e.g., headings), illustrations, and multimedia when useful to aiding comprehension.	**CCSS.ELA-LITERACY.W.6.8:** Gather relevant information from multiple print and digital sources; assess the credibility of each source; and quote or paraphrase the data and conclusions of others while avoiding plagiarism and providing basic bibliographic information for sources.
CCSS.ELA-LITERACY.W.3.7: Conduct short research projects that build knowledge about a topic.	**CCSS.ELA-LITERACY. W.4.9:** Draw evidence from literary or informational texts to support analysis, reflection, and research.	**CCSS.ELA-LITERACY. W.5.2.B:** Develop the topic with facts, definitions, concrete details, quotations, or other information and examples related to the topic.	**CCSS.ELA-LITERACY.W.6.1.B:** Support claim(s) with clear reasons and relevant evidence, using credible sources and demonstrating an understanding of the topic or text.
CCSS.ELA-LITERACY.W.3.8: Recall information from experiences or gather information from print and digital sources; take brief notes on sources and sort evidence into provided categories.	**CCSS.ELA-LITERACY. W.4.2:** Write informative/explanatory texts to examine a topic and convey ideas and information clearly.	**CCSS.ELA-LITERACY. W.5.9.B:** Apply grade 5 Reading standards to informational texts (e.g., "Explain how an author uses reasons and evidence to support particular points in a text, identifying which reasons and evidence support which point[s]").	**CCSS.ELA-LITERACY.W.6.8:** Gather relevant information from multiple print and digital sources; assess the credibility of each source; and quote or paraphrase the data and conclusions of others while avoiding plagiarism and providing basic bibliographic information for sources.
CCSS.ELA-LITERACY.RI.3.6: Distinguish their own point of view from that of the author of a text.	**CCSS.ELA-LITERACY. RI.4.6:** Compare and contrast a firsthand and secondhand account of the same event or topic; describe the differences in focus and the information provided.	**CCSS.ELA-LITERACY. RI.5.6:** Analyze multiple accounts of the same event or topic, noting important similarities and differences in the point of view they represent.	**CCSS.ELA-LITERACY.RI.6.6:** Determine an author's point of view or purpose in a text and explain how it is conveyed in the text.

TABLE 5.2 / **AASL Standards sample alignment with Common Core State Standards (seventh–twelfth grades)**

Shared Foundation IV. **Curate**

AASL Standards Framework for Learners	**COMMON CORE STATE STANDARDS** **English Language Arts Standards**		
	7	**8**	**9**
THINK **IV.A.1.** Learners act on an information need by determining the need to gather information.	**CCSS.ELA-LITERACY.W.7.7:** Conduct short research projects to answer a question, drawing on several sources and generating additional related, focused questions for further research and investigation.	**CCSS.ELA-LITERACY.W.8.2.B:** Develop the topic with relevant, well-chosen facts, definitions, concrete details, quotations, or other information and examples.	**CCSS.ELA-LITERACY.W.9-10.1:** Write arguments to support claims in an analysis of substantive topics or texts, using valid reasoning and relevant and sufficient evidence.
CREATE **IV.B.2.** Learners gather information appropriate to the task by collecting information representing diverse perspectives.	**CCSS.ELA-LITERACY.W.7.1.A:** Introduce claim(s), acknowledge alternate or opposing claims, and organize the reasons and evidence logically.	**CCSS.ELA-LITERACY.RI.8.9:** Analyze a case in which two or more texts provide conflicting information on the same topic and identify where the texts disagree on matters of fact or interpretation.	**CCSS.ELA-LITERACY.W.9-10.1.B:** Develop claim(s) and counterclaims fairly, supplying evidence for each while pointing out the strengths and limitations of both in a manner that anticipates the audience's knowledge level and concerns.
SHARE **IV.C.2.** Learners exchange information resources within and beyond their learning community by contributing to collaboratively constructed information sites by ethically using and reproducing others' work.	**CCSS.ELA-LITERACY.W.7.8:** Gather relevant information from multiple print and digital sources, using search terms effectively; assess the credibility and accuracy of each source; and quote or paraphrase the data and conclusions of others while avoiding plagiarism and following a standard format for citation.	**CCSS.ELA-LITERACY.W.8.8:** Gather relevant information from multiple print and digital sources, using search terms effectively; assess the credibility and accuracy of each source; and quote or paraphrase the data and conclusions of others while avoiding plagiarism and following a standard format for citation.	**CCSS.ELA-LITERACY.W.9-10.6:** Use technology, including the Internet, to produce, publish, and update individual or shared writing products, taking advantage of technology's capacity to link to other information and to display information flexibly and dynamically.
GROW **IV.D.1.** Learners select and organize information for a variety of audiences by performing ongoing analysis of and reflection on the quality, usefulness, and accuracy of curated resources.	**CCSS.ELA-LITERACY.RI.7.1:** Cite several pieces of textual evidence to support analysis of what the text says explicitly as well as inferences drawn from the text.	**CCSS.ELA-LITERACY.RI.8.9:** Analyze a case in which two or more texts provide conflicting information on the same topic and identify where the texts disagree on matters of fact or interpretation.	**CCSS.ELA-LITERACY.RI.9-10.1:** Cite strong and thorough textual evidence to support analysis of what the text says explicitly as well as inferences drawn from the text.

Source: CCSS alignment created by Len Bryan for Denver (Colorado) Public Schools.

KEY COMMITMENT: Make meaning for oneself and others by collecting, organizing, and sharing resources of personal relevance.

COMMON CORE STATE STANDARDS **English Language Arts Standards**		
10	**11**	**12**
CCSS.ELA-LITERACY.W.9-10.2: Write informative/explanatory texts to examine and convey complex ideas, concepts, and information clearly and accurately through the effective selection, organization, and analysis of content.	**CCSS.ELA-LITERACY.W.11-12.2.B:** Develop the topic thoroughly by selecting the most significant and relevant facts, extended definitions, concrete details, quotations, or other information and examples appropriate to the audience's knowledge of the topic.	**CCSS.ELA-LITERACY.W.11-12.8:** Gather relevant information from multiple authoritative print and digital sources, using advanced searches effectively; assess the strengths and limitations of each source in terms of the task, purpose, and audience; integrate information into the text selectively to maintain the flow of ideas, avoiding plagiarism and overreliance on any one source and following a standard format for citation.
CCSS.ELA-LITERACY.W.9-10.2.B: Develop the topic with well-chosen, relevant, and sufficient facts, extended definitions, concrete details, quotations, or other information and examples appropriate to the audience's knowledge of the topic.	**CCSS.ELA-LITERACY.W.11-12.8:** Gather relevant information from multiple authoritative print and digital sources, using advanced searches effectively; assess the strengths and limitations of each source in terms of the task, purpose, and audience; integrate information into the text selectively to maintain the flow of ideas, avoiding plagiarism and overreliance on any one source and following a standard format for citation.	**CCSS.ELA-LITERACY.W.11-12.9:** Draw evidence from literary or informational texts to support analysis, reflection, and research.
CCSS.ELA-LITERACY.W.9-10.8: Gather relevant information from multiple authoritative print and digital sources, using advanced searches effectively; assess the usefulness of each source in answering the research question; integrate information into the text selectively to maintain the flow of ideas, avoiding plagiarism and following a standard format for citation.	**CCSS.ELA-LITERACY.W.11-12.6:** Use technology, including the Internet, to produce, publish, and update individual or shared writing products in response to ongoing feedback, including new arguments or information.	**CCSS.ELA-LITERACY.W.11-12.6:** Use technology, including the Internet, to produce, publish, and update individual or shared writing products in response to ongoing feedback, including new arguments or information.
CCSS.ELA-LITERACY.RI.9-10.6: Determine an author's point of view or purpose in a text and analyze how an author uses rhetoric to advance that point of view or purpose.	**CCSS.ELA-LITERACY.RI.11-12.6:** Determine an author's point of view or purpose in a text in which the rhetoric is particularly effective, analyzing how style and content contribute to the power, persuasiveness, or beauty of the text.	**CCSS.ELA-LITERACY.RI.11-12.1:** Cite strong and thorough textual evidence to support analysis of what the text says explicitly as well as inferences drawn from the text, including determining where the text leaves matters uncertain.

SHARED FOUNDATION IV. **Curate**

DOMAIN		NATIONAL SCHOOL LIBRARY STANDARDS
A. THINK	**LEARNER** Competencies	Learners act on an information need by: 1. Determining the need to gather information. 2. Identifying possible sources of information. 3. Making critical choices about information sources to use.
	SCHOOL LIBRARIAN Competencies	School librarians challenge learners to act on an information need by: 1. Modeling the response to a need to gather and organize information. 2. Designing opportunities for learners to explore possible information sources. 3. Guiding learners to make critical choices about information sources to use.
	SCHOOL LIBRARY Alignments	The school library provides problem-based learning experiences and environments by: 1. Using resources and technology to foster inquiry and scaffold mastery of skills necessary for learning to progress. 2. Adopting a dynamic collection-development plan to ensure that adequate resources reflect current and in-depth knowledge. 3. Focusing on the effective use of a wide range of resources to foster information skills appropriate to content areas.
	LEARNER Competencies	Learners gather information appropriate to the task by: 1. Seeking a variety of sources. 2. Collecting information representing diverse perspectives. 3. Systematically questioning and assessing the validity and accuracy of information. 4. Organizing information by priority, topic, or other systematic scheme.

FIGURE 5.1 /
National School Library Standards **crosswalk with ISTE Standards for Students and Educators**

Using AASL Crosswalks

AASL has produced *National School Library Standards* crosswalks to various national and content-area standards, including the ISTE Standards for Students and Educators, the Future Ready Framework, the Next Generation Science Standards, Code with Google's CS First Curriculum, and ASCD Whole Child Tenets (AASL 2019a). Each crosswalk can be accessed on the AASL Standards web portal. AASL continues to review other standards for future crosswalks to the *National School Library Standards*. These tools provide additional collaborative entry points for school librarians to use with other educators and administrators to weave curation instruction into the academic experiences of learners.

	KEY COMMITMENT: Make meaning for oneself and others by collecting, organizing, and sharing resources of personal relevance.
	ISTE STANDARDS
	3. ISTE for Students: Knowledge Constructor 3c. Students curate information from digital resources using a variety of tools and methods to create collections of artifacts that demonstrate meaningful connections or conclusions.
	6. ISTE for Students: Creative Communicator 6a. Students choose the appropriate platforms and tools for meeting the desired objectives of their creation or communication. 6b. Students create original works or responsibly repurpose or remix digital resources into new creations. 6c. Students communicate complex ideas clearly and effectively by creating or using a variety of digital objects such as visualizations, models, or simulations. 6d. Students publish or present content that customizes the message and medium for their intended audiences.

Figure 5.1 is an excerpt from the crosswalk document for AASL's *National School Library Standards* and the ISTE Standards. Notice the Competency similarities between the AASL Think Domain and the ISTE Standards for learners as knowledge constructors. Notice that the *National School Library Standards* provide more detail on *how* learners curate information to make meaningful connections, *how* school librarians make this happen, and *how* school library programs support learners within the Think Domain. Crosswalks like these can be instrumental as we incorporate AASL Standards into existing curricula, units, and lessons, primarily if other educators use different standards to build their instruction. School librarians rarely teach in isolation, so being conversant in how the AASL Standards complement

other national and content-area standards is a game changer for every school librarian who wants to be an integral part of the school-wide instructional plan.

Facilitating Collaborative Curation

Teaching curation to support classroom instruction involves knowing what, how, and why educators teach. As noted, this knowledge emerges through collaborative planning with other educators. Collaboration can be challenging because of schedules, time constraints, and instructional time. Consider some strategies to help facilitate collaboration:

- Recruit volunteers to read aloud to classes, handle circulation, repair books, and shelve, thus freeing you to plan and collaborate with other educators.
- Invite educators to plan inside the school library—offer them coffee, doughnuts, and a place to spread out.
- Learn when and where educators are planning and try to be there.

These strategies connect closely to the Create and Share Domains, whereby school librarians employ curation tools to facilitate the sharing of curated collections with peers, other educators, and the community, as needed. We share our space, time, collections, and expertise with our educator partners, helping them create more robust units of study for learners.

Examples of Collaborative Curation

To help illustrate the scaffolding and curricular collaboration discussed in this chapter, here are a few ideas for collaborative curation opportunities at different grade levels and in different subject areas.

ELEMENTARY SCHOOL

Science fairs offer school librarians excellent opportunities to collaborate and model the Curate Shared Foundation by providing curated resources to support learners' work, spaces for learner teams to spread out and collaborate, and opportunities to connect learner projects to the world outside the classroom. Community connections require school librarians to use curation skills. We must conduct research, evaluate the potential of a partnership, and create and then maintain a mutually beneficial relationship with at least one contact within the community-based organization. This work aligns closely with the Create Domain because the tools and resources, along with professional knowledge, to locate, assess, and collect materials that benefit learners are related to the curriculum. Create connections with people and organizations that take a special interest in learners' work and that take part in events like the science fair as judges, advisors, or sponsors, or in other roles.

Scaffolding in the elementary school context can be done by grade level. For example, learners may compete in a school-wide science fair in third grade. In that case, those learners may benefit from guest speakers from community organizations who can talk about their jobs and how their jobs use science every day. Learners can then be guided toward school library resources that help them learn more about careers and the science that supports them. The same approach can be taken for older learners, with less guidance toward specific careers and more freedom for them to pursue their scientific interests.

FIELD NOTE **Connecting with Public Librarians**

The collaborative relationship school librarians have with public librarians can influence the culture of literacy in the community. The school district I work for partners closely with the public library system to plan and host the annual North Texas Teen Book festival. Over the years, I have had many opportunities to host panels where popular middle grade and young adult authors discuss their works, perspectives, and journeys to success. Since the festival is in our community, the school librarians in my district always make it a point to encourage learners to attend, and some even offer to take students as part of a field trip.

—Stacie Milburn (high school librarian, Texas)

MIDDLE SCHOOL

In middle school, learners often lose interest in self-directed reading, and it is vital to redouble efforts to ensure that books remain central to their lives. Focus on collaborating with educator partners in social studies to provide curated resources that support instruction. Many learners also begin gravitating toward specialized areas of interest, and art classes provide great opportunities to curate resources for educators and learners. Providing gallery space on top of school library shelves or partnering with an art educator to provide unique programming are two examples of curation. Curation is not always about collecting *things* for learners; it can often mean collecting and sharing *experiences* with learners.

Scaffolding learners' curation work at the middle school level is both easier and more complex than at the elementary level. It is easier because most learners now study discrete subjects with educators who are dedicated to those subjects. Curation in discrete subjects is narrower in scope than attempting to cover multiple objectives simultaneously.

Conversely, curation at the middle school level can be more challenging because it becomes even more important for school librarians to help learners connect disparate subjects to understand the world around them coherently. A common pitfall when working with learners at this level is to assume that they have developed the skills for research and curation. Consider scaffolding with the youngest middle school learners, assuming they know little about locating, assessing, and using information resources. Some middle schools have access to resources, like databases, that learners have not previously accessed. In working with learners and other educators over the middle school years, school librarians should place increased emphasis on skills such as citing sources in the proper format and creating bibliographies and works cited pages. These skills serve as excellent places to scaffold instruction.

HIGH SCHOOL

As learners enter high school, their transition provides fertile ground for teaching them how to curate resources, relationships, and experiences. Learn about the interests within your school community. Tap into them to redefine the school library as *the* place to explore those passions. Then ensure that your collection supports multiple areas of interest. For example, specialized collections may be curated to feature popular school clubs, athletics programs, hobbies, and careers.

Scaffolding curation work for high school learners can be very complex, mostly because of the differences in educator expectations, diverging learner interests, and the pressure of ensuring that learners are college and career ready when they graduate. It can be beneficial for high school campuses to reach a consensus on citation style to streamline learning and instruction for learners and educators. Although all departments are essential for instruction, collaborating with the English department is beneficial. School librarians also can effectively scaffold curation instruction by helping their campuses and districts streamline their electronic tools, such as learning management systems (LMSs) and their cloud productivity/storage solutions. Typical examples are Microsoft or Google products. Scaffolding is most effective when learners (and educators) do not have to adjust to multiple platforms throughout their high school experience.

As for curation work, it is helpful to work closely with high school English educators for several reasons. First, English is required for all learners in all grades, with few exceptions. Second, most English classes incorporate research. Finally, many curation skills that learners need are aligned with the objectives that English educators must cover. Again, approach scaffolding assuming that first-year students know little or nothing about curation.

FIELD NOTE **Connecting with Educators and Parents**

At the beginning of the year, I meet with classroom educators by grade level and tell them what I do, how we can work together, and so on. At this presentation, I remind them of where our online resources are. Last year, I sent weekly infographics that introduced one online resource at a time in an easy-to-read format. I also met with classroom educators when research units came around to plan lessons with their classes using our online databases. We started community library nights this past year and would show parents our online resources and give them a password printout so they could sign in at home. In library lessons, we explored some of our online resources with learners as a whole-class activity and as individual activities.

—Vanessa Rivas Clouston (bilingual elementary school librarian, Texas)

Using the Domains as a Guide

The Domains in the AASL Standards Frameworks offer school librarians an excellent guide in identifying opportunities for curation instruction and for learners to dive deeper and build Competencies in the Curate Shared Foundation. School librarians and learners can approach the AASL Standards at a point that fits their learning needs. However, scaffolding can happen within a lesson as learners progress through the Domains, building competency in *Think* while progressing through *Create*, *Share*, and *Grow*.

As you use the Domains as a guide, consider how you can support the needs of learners and their educators. Learners may visit the library for recreational reading or to access materials to support their assignments. However, capturing the hearts of other educators will lead to their wanting to bring learners to the library instead of sending them for brief visits. Instructional time is precious, and educators need to know that their time spent with learners will be optimized. Therefore, suggest collaborative ideas to support the curriculum and maximize learner access to the school library.

Think

As school librarians help learners determine a need for gathering information, the Think Domain helps librarians investigate learners' interests. Interests provide intrinsic motivation for learners to connect to the research process. Self-selecting research topics can help. As you work with learners to identify sources of information, encourage them to explore resources both within and outside the school library collection. Arm learners with the tools to help them make critical choices about creditable information sources.

Collaborate with other educators to develop projects incorporating learner interests. For example, a collaborative social studies lesson about essential workers could lead to learners developing a set of questions about what it means to be an essential worker during times of crisis. Educators and school librarians can collaborate to develop an event in which community members present to learners. During the presentation, learners can ask questions about their knowledge gaps. School librarians and educators can become facilitators who help learners experience meaningful learning opportunities.

Create

As school librarians move learners to the Create Domain, a common pitfall is that learners select one or two easily identified sources. Work with educator partners to ensure that learners are assessed for incorporating various sources into their work and for ensuring that those sources represent a variety of perspectives. The collaboration will move learners beyond the traditional "hunting and gathering" research approach, whereby they collect and quote or paraphrase what others have written about a subject, to an analytical approach, whereby they actively seek divergent views and include those views in their work.

As learners develop Competencies in this Domain, school librarians can interact with learners to assess, organize, and store the information they find. The SIFT method and RADAR Framework questions provided in chapter 3 are great ways to introduce learners to these Competencies. Demonstrate how information can be organized by priority, chronologically, or by topic. Instruction in outlining, storyboarding, or other methods suitable to the specifics of assignments is excellent for applying these skills.

Share

Within the Share Domain, learners communicate their knowledge within and outside their classrooms and schools. School librarians frequently have strong community connections and are perfect conduits for moving learning outside the school walls. School librarians create professional learning communities that may include authors, experts in various fields, and community members outside the school building. Leverage these ties to help learners access and evaluate collaboratively constructed information sites, ethically contribute to these sites, and collaborate with others to evaluate the results of their learning, as compared and contrasted with these resources found outside school. These exercises help learners see strong connections between their academic pursuits and the world outside their classrooms and schools.

Grow

It is in the Grow Domain that school librarians guide learners to develop a nuanced understanding of curation for different purposes and audiences. As learners build curation skills, ensure that they add to their database with each grade level. Coordinating this process with other educators will ensure that learners will have databases with background knowledge to support them throughout their primary and secondary school experiences. As learners gain experience, please encourage them to analyze and reflect on the quality and usefulness of curated resources. They may compare the resources they have chosen, the resources their classroom educators have selected, and the resources available in the school library. As learners' skills advance, help them understand that human knowledge is connected and that these conceptual knowledge networks are added to, modified, and adapted to suit learners' needs and the needs of others. Learners become a part of the global knowledge network as they contribute and gain understanding. Finally, work with learners to help them become comfortable with vulnerability by openly communicating their curation processes for others to build upon. Learners can practice communicating their use of citations, their search and assessment methods, and how they have structured their learning products as they take their places within the networks of human knowledge.

Customizing the Curate Shared Foundation for Your Learners

In this chapter, we have provided two methods for customizing the Curate Shared Foundation. The first strategy is to use scaffolding. It has been established that the Curate Shared Foundation applies to all school levels. You can apply the Competencies to your instructional practices in elementary, middle, or high schools. However, your learners' needs and skill sets will dictate the methods to differentiate instruction through scaffolding. Although scaffolding is critical for learners in the early stages of skill development, eventually scaffolds can be removed or adjusted.

A second method for customizing the Curate Shared Foundation is to use the standard crosswalks developed by AASL. These crosswalks provide examples of what learning should be like for various grade levels. Moreover, they indicate how the curation skills taught in the school library are integrated with the broader school curriculum. Think of the crosswalks as guides for instruction and an advocacy tool for initiating and maintaining collaborative instructional relationships. As you implement the crosswalks and review how the competencies fit within the curriculum, use them to identify opportunities for curation instruction. Combining scaffolding techniques and the creative implementation of the AASL crosswalks will facilitate collaborative programming and instruction to enhance learners' educational experiences.

Questions for the Reflective Practitioner

1. What connections exist between the Curate Shared Foundation and other national or content-area education standards critical to my school's mission?
2. Which standards crosswalk documents may be most helpful to me in working with other educators in my school to scaffold curation instruction with learners? What existing collaborative lessons do I teach that could incorporate more scaffolding?
3. How can I better facilitate my time during or after school or make my school library space more welcoming to promote and plan collaborative lessons with other educators?

PART III

Beyond Books

6

Curating with and for School Communities

The school library collection is central to school library services, and developing the collection has traditionally been a strength of school librarians. In the past, collection development has focused on books and other print materials. School librarianship has rapidly evolved, and the paradigm has shifted to include many resources to enhance learning. School librarianship has transformed to address unique school library collections that serve as mirrors, windows, and sliding glass doors (Bishop 1990). As school librarians address mirrors, collections now consider authors beyond those embraced by large publishing companies.

Given the need for diversity, collections must include resources for learners with disabilities and learners who speak various languages. AASL (2018, p. 247) asserts that the school community should not be constrained by policies that purposely resist diverse issues, including political, economic, religious, social, ethnic, and sexual content. The art and skill of school library collection development are refined over years of education, professional development, experience, and trial and error. Fortunately, our *National School Library Standards* capture many aspects of best practices in collection development, found mainly within the Curate Shared Foundation.

Although the school library collection has historically been and will continue to be a central component of our work, our foundational curation task is curating relationships. In chapter 2, we explored how many professions rely on relationships to be successful. We must get to know our markets well, establish ourselves as trusted professionals, and provide excellent customer service if we want to thrive in our work. These efforts demand that we work hard to form strong relationships with learners, other educators, and community members.

Fostering Curation with Relationships

These ideas will help you develop relationships. They focus on being a visible, knowledgeable, and interactive information specialist.

- Engage in school-wide planning and be present at school events. If possible, ask for time to speak.
- Create a school library council that includes learners, parents, and educators to assist with curation.
- Gather the names and contact information of experts who can present at programs in the school library.
- Host professional development opportunities, both virtual and face-to-face, tailored for learners, parents, and educators to use curated digital resources and tools.
- Host a yearly orientation for your community groups to tell them about your school library policies and resources.
- Develop clubs for learners that support the curriculum and engage them with curated resources.
- Curate lessons that you and classroom educators can implement together.

Curating for Communities Beyond Books

Understanding the needs of your community will facilitate collection development. According to the *National School Library Standards*, "the school library promotes selection of appropriate resources and tools for information use" (AASL 2018, School Library IV.B.). After you know your school community thoroughly, consider aspects like balancing print and digital resources, subscribing to commercial databases, curating community resources, and making OERs available. After these resources are curated, school librarians must provide learning experiences to explain how the resources can be used.

Understand your community's needs by talking with school administrators to learn their strategic goals for the year and how they envision you supporting those goals (Cellucci and Harland 2022). Next, develop a plan showing how you can assist with each goal. The plan does not need to be complicated. A chart showing each objective, your planned activity, and the expected completion date is sufficient. Present your plan to your school administrators and provide periodic updates. Always document your success.

Another way to understand needs is to review data. Data come in many forms. For instance, census data are frequently overlooked. Examine the demographics of the school community. Typical neighborhood schools frequently have learners who walk to school, whereas magnet and charter schools allow learners to come from outside the neighborhood. If you work in a charter or magnet program that buses in learners, you can request the data from your administrator.

Patterns of school library use also provide data (Oddone 2021). For instance, what questions are asked most frequently during reference interviews? What do your classroom educators request the most each year? What section of the school library do learners browse the most? Start by reviewing checkout statistics. Then consider other ways that learners are using the library. For instance, they could spend time at the makerspace or printing 3-D images. Similarly, learners may not be checking out books. Instead, they may read in the school library and leave books on the tables. These activities count as usage.

Learners and other educators may feel more inclined to leave honest feedback when they can be anonymous. You can develop surveys by using tools such as Google Forms. Create surveys about resource needs and school library programming experiences. Exit tickets focusing on needs after a class can provide fruitful data, too. If you actively listen to and communicate with your school community and articulate their needs through curation, they will respond positively. Classroom educators and learners like to know that their school librarian values their opinion.

PHYSICAL RESOURCES

Streaming media are readily available, and balancing print and digital resources can be a concern. Media stored in several physical formats, including print and DVDs, are included in this conversation. It is essential to consider the value of your physical media against their acquisition cost, amount of use, storage requirements, and suitability of format for a school community. For example, learners in a school with a one-to-one laptop program that provides Internet access to digital materials at home may be well suited to using online materials. There is no magic formula to determine whether a specific physical format is outdated, whether the material's content is still relevant, and whether the supporting equipment is functional. As you assess the balance of your collection, consider that nonfiction in the following content areas needs to be updated frequently:

1. Science and technology
2. Social issues
3. Geography
4. Sports books focusing on specific players or teams
5. Collective and individual biographies of politicians

SUBSCRIPTION DATABASES

Another consideration as you balance your collection's print and digital aspects is the topics that various subscription databases cover. Subscription databases are updated daily by subject experts and can generally be relied upon to provide timely, relevant, age-appropriate content. As you teach your educators and learners about the many advantages of databases and their usefulness, you may see a drop in your print nonfiction collection usage. This usage decline is an excellent result because educators and learners can access databases 24-7. Their learning does not end when the school bell rings and is not bound by the limited information in print.

Database funding is always a concern because quality resources can be expensive. Several states provide free or reduced-cost databases for K–12 schools. Public libraries often share access to their databases in partnership with database vendors. If your state library or education agency does not provide access to these resources, advocate for them to start. Access to authoritative, ad-free, professionally curated digital content supports equity. Pairing advocacy with 1:1 initiatives and Bring Your Own Device (BYOD) programs assists with decreasing the digital divide. Students can learn to use rich academic resources previously available only to wealthy school districts.

CURATING COMMUNITY RESOURCES

Community resources can take a variety of forms. For instance, if you are curating items for your makerspace, your community may help you acquire the supplies. When curating physical resources for your school, create lists of needed items and share them in the school newspaper, announcements, and newsletters. People can also be community resources (Kowalski 2022). Curate a list of contacts who can help you with different tasks. For instance, if you need to advertise an event, invite a local journalist or reporter to share the news. Develop a connection with the public library. When your learners are off campus, they often have access to the public library. Collaborating with a public librarian means sharing textbooks and lists of books your learners need. The public librarian may offer complementary programming and purchase books for learners to use when they are not in school (Moreland and Kammer 2020). Each organization or group of people may enhance the school library program by providing expertise and links to new resources, experiences, and materials (Kowalski 2022). Here is a brief list of community services to help you think about the community stakeholders who may be resources:

- Churches
- Parent-teacher organization or association
- Local nonprofits
- Parents, grandparents, and guardians
- Urban League
- Academic and public libraries
- Museums
- Art galleries
- Archives
- Local orchestra or band
- Politicians and public figures
- Universities
- Small businesses

OPEN EDUCATIONAL RESOURCES

Several educational resources are available in the public domain or with a special license to allow educators to use them for teaching. These resources are frequently adaptable and can substitute for other educational resources when there is a budget to consider (Katz 2020). Another indispensable feature of OERs is that, besides being available for use, they frequently have licenses that allow users to modify and reshare them. These resources are typically associated with state or Common Core standards, making it easier to adapt them for lesson planning. Although OERs are free, sometimes they require users to give attribution to the original developer of the resource. A Creative Commons license is often attached to these resources. These sources can be excellent in school environments because there is such a focus on teaching with standards and budgeting appropriately. These resources are flexible and available on demand. An example of a website with OER lessons is OER Commons (oercommons.org).

Six Active Learning Spaces Your School Library Should Have

Active learning spaces support problem-based learning, aid in the selection of appropriate resources and tools, assist with contribution and exchange of information, and help learners explore resources. Here are six active learning spaces to curate in your school library:

1. *Small-group areas:* In your school library, make sure that you have areas available where small groups of learners can meet, talk, and brainstorm. These spaces may look like a row of diner booths on one wall, whiteboard tables for brainstorming, or teaming tables with a monitor to share device screens. It's all about what works best for your space and your learners.
2. *Large-group areas:* Most school libraries have a large-group area. Advocate for flexible furnishings in this area. Reconfigurable furniture in your large-group area will help transition the space for different styles of teaching and learning. Create an easy-to-use presentation setup. Ideally, this space should always have a projector, laptop, and screen ready to go. If possible, have multiple large-group areas that accommodate multiple classes and learning styles.
3. *Community area:* Often, the community area will be the same as the large-group area. If your school library doesn't have an auditorium or multipurpose room, more than likely your large-group area will also be where you host special events like author visits, bookfairs, and parent meetings. Therefore, flexible furniture is crucial for making your learning space truly active.

(continued)

4. *Technology-rich area:* Your school library should have a space where learners can utilize technology. Try to think beyond the basic computer lab or computer stations. Additional services include providing tablets to check out, purchasing a high-powered computer for photo editing, and creating a small music studio in an old storage room where learners can record podcasts, music, and spoken word poetry. Rethink how you can provide technology experiences that learners don't already have access to.
5. *Quiet, solitary areas:* School libraries are active environments that are no longer quiet. Still, we need to find a way to serve learners who want a place to lose themselves in a book. Try to designate a quiet room or zone. Look into creating "cave" spaces by rearranging furniture or providing screens or dividers to help learners feel more solitary. For example, rearrange floor shelving units to create mini caves in the fiction section. It won't be perfectly quiet, but it does provide a good solitary space for learners who need it.
6. *Makerspaces*: Makerspaces are diverse, ranging from a bin of LEGOs on a table in the corner to a full-blown fab lab with 3-D printers and laser cutters. How it comes together in your space depends on you and your learners and what works best. Try to give learners access to hands-on materials where they can explore new ideas and have creative play experiences. This might be a LEGO wall, a whiteboard wall, or an arts-and-crafts supply cart. Whatever it is, make sure you have a place for creativity in your school library.

How do the six active learning spaces manifest themselves in your school library? Is there a space that's missing that you need to work on?

Source: Adapted from Diana Rendina (2016, January 27), "6 Active Learning Spaces Your Library Should Have," *Knowledge Quest*, knowledgequest.aasl.org/6-active-learning-spaces-library.

Facilitating Creative Curation through the Domains

How does the school library as a place support learning under the Curate Shared Foundation? According to our Common Beliefs (AASL 2018, 11), "the school library is a unique and essential part of a learning community." Hence, the school library with a virtual and physical presence is a unifying force that serves as a nurturing space for developing curation skills. The development of these skills requires the provision of engaging programming that acknowledges that intellectual freedom is a right for every learner (AASL 2018, 11). Programming that supports intellectual freedom and creates a space for academic success and personal knowledge acquisition includes diverse materials and advocates for equitable access. Hence, the Domains in the *AASL Standards Framework for School Libraries* align with providing the resources and assistance necessary for learners to mature into productive members of society.

Think

The school library provides problem-based learning experiences and environments by using resources and technology to foster inquiry and scaffold mastery of skills necessary for learning to progress (School Library IV.A.1.). Makerspaces are great for fostering inquiry and scaffolding skills (Einarsson and Hertzum 2020). An inexpensive way to start hands-on tinkering is through breakerspaces. In breakerspaces, learners disassemble devices to see how they work and then repurpose the parts in new inventions. Ask your community to donate old electronics, toys, appliances, gadgets, tools, and storage containers. You may find old electronics at thrift stores, too. Learners can find out how electronics work, how to repurpose them for new devices, and how circuitry works. Breakerspaces are great for learners beginning at about fourth grade because of safety concerns. You can learn more about breakerspaces at nsta.org/blog/building-stem-knowledge-breakerspace.

The school library provides problem-based learning experiences and environments by adopting a dynamic collection-development plan to ensure that adequate resources reflect current and in-depth knowledge (School Library IV.A.2.). A dynamic collection-development plan can be part of the overall collection-development policy when the policy is written with broad language and does not mention specific formats. For example, Donham and Sims (2020) mention that textbooks offer learners limited viewpoints and do not provide differentiated text to support reading. Conversely, collecting materials introduces learners to various sources to support projects.

Does your policy contain words like *laser disc, videotape, CD-ROM,* or other outdated language? Replace those terms with *resource(s)* and avoid specifying the format. Updating terms will allow you to collect a more comprehensive array of formats without constantly updating your policy. A dynamic collection-development plan also ensures that school librarians evaluate the collection and make acquisitions that support the community and the curriculum to ensure diverse representation.

The school library provides problem-based learning experiences and environments by focusing on the effective use of a wide range of resources to foster information skills appropriate to content areas (School Library IV.A.3.). School librarians often excel at providing a "wide range of resources." Resources are available in multiple formats and may include tools, sewing supplies, duct tape, media of all types, gaming consoles (new and classic), phone chargers, websites, people, lists, and any object that educators or learners might need. When considering collection development to meet users' needs, start by assessing the needs of your school community. Surveys, focus groups, and a suggestion box at the school library's door can effectively gather feedback. In addition, don't forget to look at the data that have been presented in test results. What are the deficits in learning?

Moreover, what tools are necessary to shore up learning? Audit the collection to find out how old the print resources are. School librarians often overlook the benefit of having a school library committee to inform curation behaviors. A school library committee can encompass administrators, teacher's aides, reading and technology coaches, specialized educators such as special education and English learner teachers, parents, classroom educators, and learners. Each group will provide a unique perspective essential to understanding collection needs. You will better understand how to effectively curate and connect resources to the curriculum by assessing your data and communicating with your stakeholders.

Create

The school library promotes selection of appropriate resources and tools for information use by demonstrating and documenting how resources and technology are used to address information needs (School Library IV.B.1.). School libraries must have structures in place for collaborating with classroom educators to integrate resources and technology into units of study (Brown 2020). "Library time" should not be seen as a special event. Instead, it is a time for hands-on activities and for practicing skills that will enhance learners' lives. Always share how school library programming has supported the school curriculum, "demonstrating and documenting how resources and technology are used to address information needs."

You can actively show and document resources and technology. For instance, school librarians can gather and report quantitative and qualitative data about resources and tools (Oddone 2021). Connecting the use of school library tools to the needs of learners and the school community shows how the school library supports the school's mission. Collecting and reporting data can definitively evidence growth because of instruction. For example, monthly database use can be tracked before and after providing professional development or classes for connecting databases to the curriculum. Submit reports to administrators. Don't stop at your building-level administrators. Surprise your superintendent with the results, too. Provide graphs and charts to illustrate instances in which teaching a specific resource increased use. Remember that usage may do more than just spike. Usage can reach new plateaus as educators and learners grow accustomed to using a resource.

Another way to demonstrate how technology and resources are used is to highlight learners' work in the school library newsletter or morning program. Many school librarians also post examples of learners' work on the library website and in the school library. Learners can be one of the best advocates for the school library. They will become more interested in tools that other learners have used. When learners are successful, they like to brag about their work. Be sure to place examples of learners' work in your yearly portfolio. See Appendix H, "Evidence of Accomplishment," in the *National School Library Standards* (AASL 2018) for examples of documents that can be curated to authenticate the impact of the school library. Because Appendix H centers on evidence, advertising examples of the products produced and the school library materials used to create those products validates for learners and other educators how library resources can be used for their information needs.

The school library promotes selection of appropriate resources and tools for information use by providing opportunities for all members of the school community to develop information and technology skills needed to promote the transfer of information-related problem-solving strategies across all disciplines (School Library IV.B.2.). Programming related to technology skills can be a fun, rewarding experience for school librarians, learners, other educators, and the community. This programming could be teen-grandparent or senior programs in which teens teach media skills. Some school librarians host a Genius Bar in the school library where student volunteers help other learners, staff, or community members with their technology issues (Paul 2021). A Lunch and Learn series in which educators present drop-in workshops for other educators can be effective. Sit with colleagues and offer help or advice about anything they need. Other possibilities include evening programs for caregivers on online safety, digital citizenship, and cybersecurity. Remember, you do not need to do all the work yourself. Many community members, such as retirees, stay-at-home parents, college students, and business owners, may host workshops and help educators and learners troubleshoot technology. We also have colleagues in public libraries. They can be superb partners, with more flexibility for providing learning opportunities during afterschool hours. Many of them coordinate enrichment programs.

Teaching technology skills transfers across disciplines because technology is threaded throughout society. Learners who cannot use technology will experience a lower quality of life because of the inaccessibility of information. It is likely that when a new tool is adopted, it will affect all curriculum areas. Librarians can help their communities adjust to technology adoption initiatives. Research shows that classroom educators appreciate when school librarians are available to provide tutorials and hands-on training (Smith et al., 2022). The same study further suggests that classroom instruction is hindered when learners do not have the foundational skills to use adopted technologies. As a result, educators welcome the idea of school librarians teaching technology skills to learners.

The school library promotes selection of appropriate resources and tools for information use by employing a dynamic collection policy that includes selection and retention criteria for all materials within the collection (School Library IV.B.3.). Revisit school library policies regularly, especially as privacy practices shift. Expand the definition of school library materials to include emerging technologies and diverse voices. Here, most school libraries do well with establishing selection criteria. Many do not, however, create strong retention policies and the related weeding practices and policies that help school libraries succeed. It can be difficult to weed the collection and discard the weeded books without inviting public scrutiny. One way to prevent such scrutiny is to invite educators and the community to learn about this aspect of collection development. It is also a great way to build relationships, expand your school library allies, and even recruit volunteers to help with the tremendous work.

The school library promotes selection of appropriate resources and tools for information use by implementing an administratively approved and endorsed policy that clearly addresses procedures for handling material challenges (School Library IV.B.4.). Include community involvement in material selection, review, and disposition by creating a school library advisory board (Hughes-Hassell 2020). Your advisory board can include classroom educators, paraprofessionals, administrators, parents, learners, and at least one community member. Involving many perspectives in collection development makes responding to challenges less daunting because more people own the selection processes. People who are familiar with the school library are its very best advocates. Curating relationships with campus and district administrators also ensures that no one is excluded from the development and execution of a material challenge policy.

Carefully curating relationships between the school librarian, parents, and guardians helps during challenges. Parents should know the school librarian personally. Then they can vouch for the school librarian's intentions and devotion to learners. Building relationships means challenges are less likely to be contentious.

The school library promotes selection of appropriate resources and tools for information use by designing and providing adequate, appropriate space for library resources, services, and activities (School Library IV.B.5.). As we diversify our school library collections to include more digital resources, we may need less shelf space for printed books. If a remodel or renovation is on the horizon, consider the Learning Commons model—less space for stuff and stacks and more space for learner collaboration.

In her blog post for *School Library Journal,* Joyce Valenza (2008) recommended that school librarians shift their perspectives to consider how people use libraries. It is essential to go beyond a grocery store model for services (i.e., a place where people go to get things). Instead, compare school libraries to a kitchen (i.e., a place to make things, gather, and make a mess). Table 6.1 offers examples of products for creation in a curation kitchen. Since Valenza's post, acceptance of an active school

TABLE 6.1 / **Curation in the school library kitchen**

Things We Do	Products for Creation
Make new recipes	Digital stories Computer code Makerspace projects Films Websites
Gather ingredients	Ideas Books Digital resources Friends and colleagues New perspectives
Savor experiences	Bookfairs Art shows Human library interviews Tournaments Hackathons

library for "making" has increased. Now school librarians are carefully curating experiences, services, and activities for their users that create the school library as a safe "third space," a physically, mentally, and emotionally safe space. School libraries are a space where educators and learners can gather without pressure to buy products, complete a task, or embody a persona that is not theirs.

Share

The school library facilitates the contribution and exchange of information within and among learning communities by providing an environment in which resources that support the school's curriculum and learning goals can be collaboratively selected and developed (School Library IV.C.1.). Establish an advisory board comprising learners, staff members, parents, administrators, and the community to provide input and feedback on priorities (AASL 2018, 101). The learner's voice is a critical component of this practice. Work with other educators and community members to regularly assess the collection and its applicability to the curricula. Consistently ask for input on collection-development choices, such as books, websites, and other learning tools that may be useful in classes and beyond. Try to serve on textbook or curriculum adoption committees, or both. Very few people in a school know the various curricula as well as the school librarian. Leverage that knowledge to become the go-to resource for understanding how different grade-level and subject-area studies can fit together into a coherent experience for learners as they matriculate through school.

The school library facilitates the contribution and exchange of information within and among learning communities by including and tracking collection materials in a system that uses standardized approaches to description and location (School Library IV.C.2.). Consider potential reporting features and pitfalls when setting up or changing the structure of information in MARC records or within your integrated library system (ILS). Call numbers, genre fields, and sublocations can be useful in reporting how specific parts of the collection are used. Running reports filtered by this information can yield more insight than a simple circulation report.

Speaking of call numbers, we should address genrefication. Genrefication has been around long enough to be a common practice among school and public libraries. There is a growing trend toward genrefication that may cause unintentional harm to learners. When fiction is genrefied, librarians move roughly half a collection and classify it so readers can easily find books that appeal to them. Categories often include humor, adventure, romance, horror, and more.

Academic libraries also genrefy, to a lesser degree, by providing access to special collections geared toward specific disciplines. Departing from the established, standard classification schemes, such as the Dewey Decimal Classification system, decreases opportunities to teach learners the importance of organization. How we apply that organizational schema in school libraries reflects how other libraries are organized. It is possible to increase access to books without creating shelving nightmares for volunteers, headaches for interlibrary loans, and call number catastrophes for whoever inherits a school library. Genrefied classifications are not standardized and may do a disservice to the learners who will need to use traditional classification systems in public and university libraries.

The school library facilitates the contribution and exchange of information within and among learning communities by establishing policies that promote effective acquisition, description, circulation, sharing, and access to resources within and beyond the school day (School Library IV.C.3.). Acquisitions can be enhanced tremendously by diversifying vendor relationships. Many districts have agreements with vendors that specify discounts, free shipping, processing, and MARC records. Besides working with large school library jobbers for purchases, consider contacting niche vendors for diverse titles. Diversity ideas include acquiring books in specific languages and varied author voices to provide an excellent reading experience for learners. Policies such as interlibrary loan may already be in place in your district or region. If they are not, joining a consortium to share books is an extensive task worth the effort.

Removing barriers such as authentication for digital resources is also an excellent investment. Consider working with your vendors to provide URLs that have credentials embedded. You can also use IP address authentication to ensure that users are not prompted for passwords within your district networks. Review geolocation and other technologies that facilitate access, such as Ezproxy. If your district uses a single sign-on authentication method, ensure that school library resources are included. Also ensure that OPAC and online resources are available to learners 24-7 so users can engage with resources, make suggestions, and request assistance (AASL 2018, 101).

FIELD NOTE **Finding Credible Book Reviews**

Librarians can access the JLG [Junior Library Guild] website and choose which categories they want to purchase. When thinking about books that I want to add to my collection, I am concerned about things such as explicit language. JLG identifies which of the books within the category I have chosen have the concerns that I have denoted. This

(continued)

identification helps me to easily see if it would be appropriate for the school library or if I need to switch the book for another book before it is sent to me. Amazingly enough, 80 to 90 percent of the books JLG recommends end up being best sellers or award winners. JLG has been especially helpful because I manage an international school library, and I cannot use Follett Titlewave anymore because shipping costs have increased. Besides collection development, school librarians have a lot of other work, like setting up programs, teaching classes, circulation, and book processing, and because of this, getting assistance with this aspect of collection development is helpful from services like JLG, which carefully finds the best and newest books available.

—Christina Stowers (K–12 school librarian, Kaohsiung, Taiwan)

The school library facilitates the contribution and exchange of information within and among learning communities by maintaining procedures that ensure user confidentiality and promote unimpeded access to materials by staff members and learners (School Librarian IV.C.4.). Volunteer and learner use of your OPAC and ILS can be constructive because it frees school librarians from clerical circulation tasks. However, avoiding proper precautions can put users' information at risk. Work with your system administrator to ensure that credentials given to student aides or library volunteers do not allow for viewing a learner's personal information, checkout history, or other sensitive content. Setting up and providing self-checkout to help protect privacy is a terrific option to allow users unfettered access to the school library collection. With self-checkout, no human needs to see what the user has checked out. It is also possible in many ILSs to set up a self-check-in station, further protecting users' privacy and reducing the school librarian's workload. As we work to curate relationships with our learners, protecting their privacy and right to read only enhances their trust in the school library and us.

School librarians with aides or volunteers can maximize access by teaching classes and allowing learners to check out books simultaneously. Librarians can establish student library aide clubs to assist with shelving books and facilitating checkout at self-service checkout stations. A few minutes before or after school can be beneficial for allowing learners in fixed-schedule schools to have library time without interrupting their class times. For instance, special passes can allow access during these times. A little time spent at the beginning of the year to create library checkout bookmarks and teach learners how to use them can facilitate easy self-checkout throughout the year. Donham and Sims (2020) further noted that an alternative view of flexible scheduling provides a specific time for a class to go to the school library. If the class does not need instruction, they do not need to go to the school library, thus opening the library for other learners to visit freely.

Grow

The school library engages the learning community in exploring resources by describing, organizing, and promoting the collection for maximum and effective uses for multiple learning applications (School Library IV.D.1.). Align the school library collection with grade levels, subject areas, units of study, and special interests and then model that alignment by collaboratively teaching and developing guides to the collection (Hughes-Hassell 2020). For example, Collections by Destiny on the Follett Destiny Discover platform can be accessed to curate print and online resources into a single, accessible collection. These collections allow school librarians to describe and promote specific areas of the collection for specific purposes. If you don't have access to Collections by Destiny, a free Web 2.0 tool such as Wakelet can serve a similar purpose.

"Provide classroom educators and learners with frequent updates about school library resources and their potential uses" (AASL 2018, 101). Promotion can easily be done with a library website and through social media. Conduct usability testing of the school library's online presence when using websites. Promote resources in the collection online and in person. Providing frequent professional development opportunities for other educators and staff, offering classes and workshops for students, and engaging parents during parent nights are effective strategies. Host community group meetings in the school library and use the opportunity to promote services and collections. Curating relationships with learners, caregivers, educators, community groups, and other organizations is a terrific way to increase the visibility of the school library program. These ever-expanding connections strengthen the learning experience and place the school library program as an essential part of the community (Chant 2020). This placement can increase the use of library resources and their applicability to your school's mission.

The school library engages the learning community in exploring resources by maintaining a collection of sufficient breadth and currency to be pertinent to the school's program of studies (School Library IV.D.2.). Curriculum adoptions can provide an excellent opportunity to showcase the materials the school library already has to support units of study. Conversely, they are an opportunity to evaluate how well the print and digital collections support the curriculum. Consistently evaluate the diversity and utility of your collection via statistics. It is essential to survey and implement focus groups with educators and administrators about the collection materials and how they relate to the state standards and curriculum. Educators can tell you if they are able to locate materials in the collection to support their lessons. Because lesson plans and curricular needs may change from year to year, try doing a short midyear assessment to gauge the relevance of library materials.

Titlewave's collection analysis tool from Follett is an example of an in-depth analysis of entire collections and specific sections. When curriculum adoption opportunities arise, volunteer to be part of the committee or work group that makes these decisions. The school librarian has a specific place because of their interaction with the entire school community and the ability to articulate the learning resources present to support new curriculum adoption. Interacting with communities can provide an opportunity to assess gaps in materials, too. Again, building and maintaining strong relationships with educators and leaders throughout the school and district makes it more likely that the school librarian will be included in this process.

The school library engages the learning community in exploring resources by supporting access through a schedule that allows use by learners and staff at time of need (School Library IV.D.3.). Fixed or flexible schedules have a big impact on use and can vary significantly from district to district, level to level, or even school to school. Many elementary or primary schools in the United States operate on fixed schedules, whereby the school library is part of a "specials" rotation, usually along with physical education and music. The advantages of fixed schedules include consistent learner access to the school library and its collections, the potential for a coherent school library curriculum based on consistent and predictable learner contact, and significantly increased circulation from consistent learner access.

The school library space is available at the point of need with flexible scheduling. Flexible scheduling creates time in the school library's schedule for the school librarian to perform administrative tasks or other duties as needed by the school and ensures that the school library is available before school, during lunch, and after school. Flexible scheduling is also constructive because it allows extensive collaboration between the school librarian and other educators. The flexible scheduling model is most often seen in secondary schools in the United States.

Conversely, a blended model is the preferred format. At the elementary level, this model has fixed scheduling for Pre-K through second or third grade, then flexible scheduling for older learners, with the expectation that educators of older learners will schedule school library time at least once per month and collaborate with the school librarian regularly. A fully flexible school library schedule is advised for secondary school, with the expectation that language arts educators will schedule their classes for booktalks and checkout at least once per month and that educators in all subject areas will collaborate with the school librarian for at least one unit of study.

Should you encounter a fixed schedule, you can approach it with creative workarounds. Enlist the services of a well-trained volunteer parent to help you when classes are in the library. Another option is to connect classes with remote options. For instance, you can "visit" a class remotely while another class is in the library learning the same lesson. Learners can also be taught how to check out their materials by themselves. Consider writing a grant or requesting a donation from a local business to purchase a book vending machine or library checkout kiosk. Opening a few minutes before and after school may be options for your school. Torres and Tagoe (2022) noted that many librarians began offering more online programming as a result of the COVID-19 pandemic. If you use these creative options, scheduling and communicating with your school community to moderate traffic are essential.

School library staffing also affects access because there is too much work for one person to accomplish. Although the school library is often seen as a classroom, the volume of work involved in managing a school library's materials is far greater than the volume of work required to manage the materials in a classroom. Speaking from experience as a classroom educator and a school librarian, there is no comparison. Paraprofessional or clerical staffing must be in place for school librarians to be effective educators. Many classroom educators would love clerical assistance. For school librarians, this support is vital.

School librarians should use this newfound time to create and share tutorials and other supports for self-guided, independent research skills and other information-seeking activities (AASL 2018, 101). Furthermore, time can be used to meet with other educators regularly to align instruction to benefit all learners. If you are feeling adventurous, learners often welcome the surprise of seeing the school librarian visit their classrooms for conversations and brief collaborative lessons. Such activities establish the school librarian as a well-rounded educator in their eyes.

The school library engages the learning community in exploring resources by using local and external data to inform ongoing adjustments to the scope of the resource collection and its audiences, formats, and applications (School Library IV.D.4.). Data literacy is another skill that school librarians should curate within their practice. Data fuel evidence-driven practice and can help you make decisions about your collection development, access to and promotion of resources for learners, and your instruction to improve learning opportunities. In addition, data inform decisions in most schools. The existence of supporting data can impact school library funding. Curation practices present opportunities to collect and report data on all types of resources used in the school library and, more importantly, their impact on learners' experiences. Collect quantitative (the numbers) and qualitative (the stories) documentation when considering data.

Data collection and reporting can vary greatly and should align with the strategic priorities of your campus, district, region, or state. Plenty of school library data are ripe for analysis. To name a few, circulation, online resource use, classes taught, and website hits are all available.

Different decision makers have various perspectives on information. Although some might be convinced by a detailed pie chart to increase (or begin) support of the school library program, others need to hear stories about how learners use school library resources and their impact on academic achievement. Prepare yourself to tell the story of the data you have collected. Identify what your school library does well, what sets it apart from other school libraries, and how the curated resources relate to academic achievement.

Avoid confusing correlation with causality when connecting school library data to campus or district priorities. We can confidently show a connection between solid circulation numbers and improved literacy measured by test scores. However, it would be a mistake to claim one caused the other.

When deciding what metrics to measure, school librarians should ensure that each one addresses a need that is essential to the school's mission and learning initiatives. Data can be presented in myriad ways that affect their meaning and interpretation, so school librarians should be aware of how they judge the scope and usefulness of their collections by examining data over time. Using data can be especially important if you are new to a school. A new librarian may not know what initiatives a former school librarian implemented. However, the data from the collection and the school's academic achievement scores can provide a strong foundation for developing library programs. A school librarian should follow up on the quantitative data collection by using qualitative data to understand the meaning behind the numbers.

Though it will take some work to develop the data collection and analysis skills, once a robust data collection and reporting campaign is in place, collecting data can become second nature for you and, in some cases, almost automated. Consider viewing and comparing data at the building level and across the district, region, and state. The standardization of different metrics across a district, region, or state can show disparities and inequities between campuses and highlight strengths and growth areas of your campus. Data collection and reporting can become a consideration when adopting new products and services. For example, asking vendors to show what metrics they can provide about their product's use will help you determine how implementation can address learning disparities. You are highly advised not to purchase a product or service unless a data conversation is incorporated into the negotiation.

Data can inform curation decisions and can be a powerful ally in advocacy efforts. If data are the language and currency of education and are used to make choices within states and school districts, they should inform school library decisions. Therefore, the collection and reporting of data must also become a part of school library practice.

Making Data-Driven Curation Decisions

Making data-driven decisions can assist school librarians with providing the best curated materials and programs for learners. Consider these strategies for setting up your data collection efforts before the school year begins:

- Examine your district and campus vision, mission, and strategic plan. Align data collection to address *how* the school library program supports them.
- Leverage the feedback of your school library advisory board to support collection, programming, and other aspects of the school library that can help meet their needs. This practice directly supports one of our Curate Best Practices: "Create mechanisms for your collection's users to provide suggestions for new materials and provide feedback on existing materials" (AASL 2018, 101).
- Collect research on the impact of school libraries. AASL publishes a scholarly, refereed research journal, *School Library Research*, which is an excellent place to start. AASL also provides a host of other advocacy tools on its website (aasl.org).
- Set up mechanisms to collect both quantitative and qualitative data:
    - » Reports from your integrated library system on circulation, top users, top titles, and peak circulation times
    - » Database usage reports
    - » A calendar to track instruction and events
    - » Gate counter or snapshot days to count visitors to the library
    - » A suggestion box or online form for book purchases, ideas, and feedback
    - » A forum to capture book reviews (some OPACs collect this information; you can also use index cards taped to shelves, like a bookstore)
    - » Feedback surveys for lessons, programming, events, and collection evaluations
- Create a process for capturing and sharing pictures and videos of the school library and its visitors. Remember to get permission to use photos.
- Create social media accounts and track interactions and comments using a hashtag for your school library.

Curation and Considerations for the Future

We designed this chapter to lead you in a thought process focused on how the school library is essential to facilitating healthy curation practices. The possibilities are limitless for establishing a strong, meaningful, and effective school library that supports the development of curation skills. The key is to provide optimal access to collections, whether the collections consist of experiences, people, print resources, or digital materials.

Curation should include the review of data because collecting data to improve school library services and instruction is critical to evidence-based decision making (Hughes-Hassell 2020). Examining data can reveal the steps needed to improve school library access and ensure that services and materials are relevant, engaging, and accessible. Optimizing access also means that learners should have access to materials and experiences that protect their future. Data collection for improving school library services and available materials should not compromise learners' privacy. Hence, mindful curation practices consider how educators' decisions may impact learners' futures.

Questions for the Reflective Practitioner

1. How does curating good relationships impact my ability to provide meaningful services and develop solid collections for other educators and learners?
2. When I reflect on myself as a relationship builder, what "soft skills" do I need to work on? What relationship needs do I have? What can I do to spend more time in my day on relationship building?
3. How can I leverage my relationships to implement the School Library Alignments under the Curate Shared Foundation? Which relationships? Which Alignments?

7

Considering Digital Tools

It is no secret that school librarians are frequently embedded in the technology cultures of their schools (Johnston 2012; Smith et al., 2022). Sometimes the duties of school librarians overlap with those of technology educators or fill a gap in the absence of a technology educator. In those cases, school librarians become essential for ensuring that the school community understands the available technology. Furthermore, the technology educator role is embedded in the *National School Library Standards,* which implore school librarians to instruct the learning community on collecting, organizing, and sharing resources relevant to learners' information needs and personal interests (AASL 2018, 94). To effectively implement this role, school librarians must curate digital tools and teach their school communities how to select and use digital tools.

Using digital tools opens the possibility that information can be accessed inside and outside the school library, twenty-four hours a day. Therefore, this chapter discusses the school librarian's role in curating and teaching the use of digital tools. Moreover, because it is necessary to understand how to interact with different stakeholders, this chapter discusses how school librarians can approach conversations about digital tools with various stakeholders and introduce them to curation. Finally, the concept of an Academic Technology Menu (ATM) is introduced, along with suggestions for developing one in collaboration with school and district technology personnel.

Curating Digital Tools

Innovative curation for the modern era goes far beyond simply collecting information in traditional library formats such as books, magazines, and other periodicals.

School librarians can curate educational websites, apps, games, devices, parts, tools, makerspaces, materials, social media streams, databases, and digital tools for educators and learners to use to create, and so much more. This practice is reflected in our Curate Best Practice to "expose learners to a variety of digital tools to describe and organize websites, digital videos, images, and other media" (AASL 2018, 102).

Content from nontraditional school library sources can connect educators and learners to what is happening outside the school's walls. It is imperative to curate various digital and nondigital content and tools for our school communities. Expanding the concept of traditional print curation improves support for school communities.

The temporary nature of many online resources makes it challenging to curate them into permanent collections. Changing URLs, the turnover of online content creators, and publishers merging or going out of business require school librarians to check and update links to resources periodically. The following factors should be included when determining the selection of digital resources:

- Accessibility related to file formats that may be obsolete
- School district policies and procedures that facilitate and hinder access to content
- The steps that learners and educators must use to access the content
- The relation of the content to curriculum, lesson plans, or extracurricular activities
- The ability for educators to create assignments and projects that are worthy of inclusion in a learner's permanent portfolio
- The development of portable portfolios that learners can access after they change schools, leave the district, or graduate

These considerations provide opportunities for school librarians to serve as leaders and curation experts. This type of school librarian leadership potentially adds tremendous value to schools and districts. Our ability to curate and connect tools and resources with our academic disciplines helps school librarians remain indispensable to the learning communities we serve.

Fortunately for school librarians, AASL curates an annual list vetted by a committee of school library professionals. The AASL Best Digital Tools for Teaching and Learning (AASL, n.d.-a) honors websites, apps, online tools, and digital resources of exceptional value. The resources recognized by AASL foster innovation, creativity, active participation, and collaboration. They are user-friendly, web-based resources that encourage collaboration, and many are free.

The AASL Best Digital Tools for Teaching and Learning offers a powerful resource for school librarians who want to explore curation tools. Many librarian-centric blogs and websites also support curation and instruction. Additionally, AASL's Hashtag

Bank, which includes state-specific, regional, and topical chats, may be used to communicate with educator peers about their tools and resources. Resources such as these, curated by experts, form a terrific starting point in our digital resource curation journey.

Collaborating with Adult Learners

Although school librarians teach the use of curation tools independently, we also lead in the integration of digital curation tools. We work alongside our peers in the classroom to teach learners (and sometimes educators) about these tools and their usefulness in creating innovative, unique learning products. Other educators often have differing comfort levels with digital tools, making integration challenging.

How can we address different adult learners' comfort levels with curation tools and strategies when collaborating on instruction? It may be useful to view these interactions through the lens of the personas introduced in the *National School Library Standards* (AASL 2018, 20–24). More-detailed persona profiles exploring potential values, goals, and questions associated with each persona are provided on the AASL Standards web portal (AASL 2022). Familiarize yourself with these persona profiles, and customize profiles for your own community. Personas can help school librarians formulate strategies as we work with our peers to integrate digital tools and implement the Curate Shared Foundation.

NOAH WHO NEEDS SUPPORT

For school librarians matching this persona, it might be helpful to offer practical advice on how to curate, teach curation, and reflect on collection-development activities. Start with a community needs assessment—find out what curriculum areas need support and which educators want help with digital resources. Then, locate, evaluate, collect, and promote resources that meet those needs. Assess learners' needs through surveys, reference interviews, book groups, and suggestion boxes to determine areas where digital tools can be useful.

INEZ THE INNOVATOR

School librarians can be innovators and influence innovators. Innovators like Inez can be challenged to blog about and present digital tools and strategies at campus, district, state, and national events. Innovators should be encouraged to share curation best practices—both identifying exemplary digital tools and curating using digital tools—through articles, chats, and other professional connections. People like Inez are great to team up with for giving presentations and sharing success stories.

MARGOT THE MENTOR

School library mentors guide the conversation, defining best practices in curating digital tools for their schools, districts, or regions, emphasizing innovative tools and skills in collaboration with the learning communities they serve. Because mentors are often in district leadership roles, they are ideally placed to create partnerships between school libraries and the district's technology department, making the adoption and integration of digital tools seamless across the district.

ATHENA THE ACADEMIC

Collaboration with academics is an excellent way for school librarians to understand the impact of curation behaviors. Although collection development is an integral part of school librarianship, more causality research is needed to determine how school librarian instruction relates to the academic achievement of learners. Synergistically working with academics in research and publication activities is essential for advocating for innovative curation practices. The world needs to hear about how curation skills improve learning.

LEON THE LEAD LEARNER

Much like principals, school librarians serve as managers of school library programs. These programs need to support the school's and school district's mission statements and visions. School librarians can partner with administrators to leverage and support curation instruction to advance the learning culture of their schools. Collaborating with the school administration can ensure that curation instruction is embedded in the instructional routine of every grade level and subject area. School librarians can advocate for the support of school administration, thus influencing the instructional tone for the school by modeling the use of digital tools for other educators and families.

TONY THE TEACHER

School librarians can provide curation professional development and add value to classroom educators' instruction by suggesting appropriate digital tools for learners. School librarians may also collaboratively curate resources with other educators while co-teaching curation skills. Model ethical curation and sharing practices for other educators who may need examples of curation in action. Showing educators easy and practical ways to enhance their teaching through curation will transform reluctant curators into allies and instructional partners.

PATTY THE PARENT

School librarians can empower parents or guardians, as well as other community members, by curating resources and providing instruction, either in community-focused learning sessions or through sharing learning resources via the school library's social media presence(s).

Creating Academic Technology Menus

School librarians should collaborate with the school and district technology departments to approve digital tools and add them to district-supported app lists. Establishing a vetting process will also streamline the adaptation and discontinuation of tools. For example, Denver Public Schools (2016) has created the Academic Technology Menu (ATM) portal on which educators and administrators can select from district-approved and supported hardware and software. Although the district's technology department is excellent for developing such websites, establishing the need, setting standards, and recommending resources for consideration are all tasks to which school librarians are well suited. School librarians often are among the first in our districts to hear about new technology. We can try new tools with the school community and assess their applicability.

Furthermore, school librarians have an extensive professional learning community to turn to for reviews, potential uses with learners, tips, and troubleshooting assistance. School librarians are in the perfect position to create, add, or recommend removing tools, from coding to robotics to the latest devices. Creating a simple ATM involves placing resources on a hyperlinked Google Doc, which can be updated as tools are discovered or need change. This form of curation is most helpful to busy educators because it saves them time and energy in locating, evaluating, and determining potential uses for tools and resources. An advantage of a tool like an ATM is that school librarians can assess a tool's policies about learner data privacy through curation. Consider the educational needs of the school or district, learners' right to privacy, and what educational technology companies do with learner data.

However, collecting and sharing vetted digital tools are not enough. We must add value to this collection. Otherwise, all we are presenting is a list of links. We add value by

- describing the purpose of the tool,
- identifying what it can and cannot do,
- explaining the hardware and software required to use it,
- sharing potential curriculum connections or lesson ideas, and
- listing tips to get started quickly.

Fortunately, school librarians have extensive experience in creating posters, tip sheets, guides, instructional videos, and other supports to add value to curated resources. These value add-ons can be informed by school librarians' experience in collaborating with other educators, through reading the support materials on the tools' or resources' websites, through school librarians' PLNs, or even through their personal experience with using the tools. By featuring curriculum connections, ATMs can also increase the potential for technology use, bridging the gap between a "cool tool" and classroom instruction.

Finally, creating a tool like an ATM gives us a place to share our learning at conferences, in workshops, and within professional learning communities. We can be change agents within our professional networks and within our schools and districts. Curating, vetting, and adding value place school librarians in a leadership position.

Using Social Media as PLNs for Curation

Social media constitute another area in which school librarians can lead the way in their school's digital curation activities. Although sometimes viewed as sources of negativity and hate, social media's original intent (besides generating revenue) is to connect people. The curation of friends and followers, hashtags, scheduled chats with an academic focus, and opportunities created from social media connections are all areas in which school librarians can significantly enhance the experience of learners and other educators. Curating these channels helps the school community connect to others worldwide, providing a real-world audience and a forum for sharing ideas, events, and learning opportunities.

School librarians have an opportunity to model connections to a robust PLN for other educators in our schools and districts. As we build collections of social media channels for our learners, we also connect our schools more deeply with our communities. We are poised to bring together our caregivers, parents, grandparents, civic groups, and volunteer organizations through our connections forged in social media channels. Social media can serve as a "digital bulletin board," helping the larger community connect with the school, providing a sense of belonging, potential support, and channels for learners to take their lessons beyond the classroom walls and connect their learning to the community at large.

When we curate social media channels, we also create opportunities for our professional development. If we cannot attend a conference, we can still feel connected by following conference hashtags on X (formerly known as Twitter) or Instagram. By connecting with peers worldwide through social media feeds, we can become far more reflective school librarians. These connections come from carefully curating our social media feeds and following educators who we feel have something to teach us. We can develop a solid understanding of what the role of a school librarian entails and consider the innovations and changes to the profession through our connections with colleagues who are "in the trenches" and posting, blogging about, or otherwise sharing their experiences. Indeed, digital tools are rich resources that are a gateway to accessing a plethora of curriculum support and timely professional development materials.

School Librarians as Digital Curation Leaders

School libraries are often associated with an image of a woman fearlessly defending stacks of books from the dangers of prying fingers. Today, school librarians focus on getting a plethora of materials into learners' hands and minds. Materials extend well beyond printed books. Although traditional data collection is still alive, school librarians work tirelessly to curate, create, and ethically remix digital resources to supplement printed books.

This chapter describes how collecting digital resources is not an option in today's environment. If there ever was a question about the vitality of digital curation, it was answered with the onset of the COVID-19 pandemic. School districts relied heavily on digital resources, and school librarians were at the forefront of curating those resources and teaching learners how to use them. The pandemic proved that digital tools are essential to learning and showed that learners need the confidence and skills to access and use digital resources. From using social media to expertly connect with and inform learners to supporting the curriculum with innovative digital tools that provide free 24-7 access, by implementing the Curate Shared Foundation, school librarians are well equipped to serve as leaders in this realm of possibilities.

Questions for the Reflective Practitioner

1. What steps can I take to enhance my familiarity with and integration of digital tools in my school or district?
2. What impact could digital tools have on my collaborations and curation of materials for my school?
3. In what ways do I or can I model transferable attitudes, knowledge, and skills regarding digital tools with my learning community?
4. How can I identify and approach the stakeholders in my community who have different comfort levels with digital tools?

PART IV

Curate in Practice

8

Reflecting on Curate Case Studies

This chapter shares practical examples of curation connected to the Curate Shared Foundation in the *National School Library Standards*. The examples are shared to encourage reflection on how traditional and emerging curation activities connect learners to resources in thoughtful, meaningful ways. These examples provide a starting point for school librarians, school library supervisors, educators of school librarians, and pre-service school librarians.

Analyzing Collaboratively Constructed Resources

High school librarian Kimberly Johnson creates opportunities for learners to analyze how information sources are created and edited over time. In this example, Wikipedia is the information source. She directed learners in intensive analysis of Wikipedia articles to demystify how this popular information source came to be and to examine its advantages and disadvantages. Here is the process that Kimberly followed to engage learners in understanding how resources can be collaboratively constructed.

Collaboratively Constructed Resources, by Kimberly Johnson

I work closely with the AP U.S. Government classroom educator and students on analyzing a Wikipedia article. Learners "edit" articles on relevant government topics for accuracy, a neutral voice, and currency outside the Wikipedia platform. Articles are analyzed outside of Wikipedia because minors cannot edit Wikipedia.

(continued)

Before starting the project, the class discussed the positives and negatives of using Wikipedia for research. Learners noted the positive aspects of Wikipedia, like crowdsourced information, many "editors," the nonprofit host, and the ability to see references; it is free to use and includes a variety of topics. They further shared negative characteristics like the overwhelming article lengths, placement as the first results in Google Search and how the placement causes them to ignore other search results, and the questionable accuracy of information. The discussion showed they had already thought critically about using Wikipedia as a source.

Next, learners were asked to select interesting government-related topics to investigate on Wikipedia. Then they were asked to go to the View History tab for the pages they selected to review the page edits, history, editors, the time between edits, and trends in page edits. Learners compared the topics they selected and determined the pages that needed more work based on the statistics for each page. We also showed learners the Talk tab, where Wikipedia editors can discuss edits and the page content that still needed to be edited.

Learners then read their selected article to identify needed edits. Edits could improve previously written content by making it neutral, adding more recent information, or adding essential details. Or edits could fix errors. Finally, using the SIFT strategy (Stop, Investigate, Find trusted coverage, Trace to the original source), learners found and evaluated articles to use as their references in "editing" the Wikipedia articles. Throughout the process, learners worked on the Wikipedia "project" in pairs, evaluating collaboratively constructed information like real-life Wikipedia editors. Overall, they made critical choices about information sources while selecting their references.

Source: Kimberly Johnson, personal communication to Daniella LaShaun Smith (January 5, 2023).

REFLECTIONS ON ANALYZING COLLABORATIVELY CONSTRUCTED RESOURCES

Kimberly Johnson worked closely with the AP U.S. Government educator to enhance their learners' experience working with collaboratively constructed information sites, like Wikipedia. Although the phrase "collaboratively constructed information sites" usually brings to mind resources like Wikipedia, learning activities like this can help learners choose the information sources to use as they assess collaboratively constructed articles from academic journals, websites, documentaries, and a host of other media types. The described analysis prompts learners to examine how resources are created, the choices made during their creation, and how to either create similar sources themselves or build upon others' creations. These lifelong skills are beneficial.

Kimberly expertly describes how this level of curation work could only be accomplished through a working relationship with classroom educators. Her activity supported the School Library Alignments under the Think and Share Domains in the Curate Shared Foundation. "The school library facilitates the contribution and exchange of information within and among learning communities by providing an environment in which resources that support the school's curriculum and learning goals can be collaboratively selected and developed" (AASL 2018, School Library IV.C.1.). Furthermore, "the school library provides problem-based learning experiences and environments by using resources and technology to foster inquiry and scaffold mastery of skills necessary for learning to progress" (AASL 2018, School Library IV.A.1.) and focuses "on the effective use of a wide range of resources to foster information skills appropriate to content areas" (AASL 2018, School Library IV.A.3.).

Kimberly's example also connects to the School Librarian and Learner Competencies—namely, that school librarians are instrumental in contributing to and guiding "information resource exchange within and beyond the school learning community by facilitating opportunities to access and evaluate collaboratively constructed information sites" (AASL 2018, School Librarian IV.C.1.). In Kimberly's example, the learners exchanged information and worked together to "compare and contrast information derived from [a] collaboratively constructed" website (AASL 2018, Learner IV.C.3.). In the future, the skills the learners employed may transfer to college and beyond as learners seek to contribute vetted ideas in college and the workplace.

Curating Print Materials

In this example, Carolyn Foote, a district librarian, describes how school librarians curate library books for their schools. Give consideration to her thoughtfulness as she curated the information streams she used and became aware of potential new titles for her school library. She did not passively wait for opportunities to learn about new titles. Instead, Carolyn intentionally created opportunities to engage with various collection-development resources to ensure that the titles she purchases genuinely meet the needs of her learners and educators. To illustrate, Carolyn shares examples of how she identified titles.

New Ways to Find Titles, by Carolyn Foote

CONFERENCES AND JOURNALS

Conference sessions feature many upcoming titles, booktalks, or author panels. I love skimming booths at conferences for Starred Titles or other titles of interest.

(continued)

I like getting targeted flyers (best new graphic novels, social-emotional learning titles, etc.) that I can grab and go. If they come in the mail, I set them aside for ordering. I use ads in *School Library Journal* and other magazines to alert me to appealing titles. I take note of books on booklists and state award lists, and I do order many of those.

SOCIAL MEDIA AND INFLUENCERS
I also notice books recommended by influencers in our field, people like Jennifer LaGarde and Andy Plemmons. Because I know they have exemplary tastes, I pay attention to their recommendations. I notice social media posts, whether they be X (formerly known as Twitter) photos, Instagram, or Facebook comments on book titles.

E-MAIL AND NEWSLETTERS
Like some of you, I'm inundated with e-mails. Frequently, I don't have time to peruse the newsletters I sign up for. Like Book Riot, they must have a unique voice to make my "reading list." I look through catalogs at peak ordering time—particularly for nonfiction titles when trying to fill gaps. I use Amazon best seller lists and Goodreads recommendation lists as discovery tools for titles in specific categories.

LEARNER AND EDUCATOR VOICES
Titles that learners and other educators recommend always go on my ordering list. Units change yearly, so being sure I have the books they require or titles they want to read is paramount. We keep a suggestion line open for learners and send periodic requests to educators for new titles they would like us to add. We want to create a culture that feels communal in terms of purchasing.

Source: Adapted from Foote, 2019.

REFLECTIONS ON CURATING PRINT MATERIALS

Carolyn Foote took a self-reflective approach to her practice of curation for print sources for the school library. Taking the time to examine behaviors closely is vital, primarily as we work to make print resources more diverse, appealing, and accessible. As we acquire titles for collections, we should pause to consider our actions. Don't rush to purchase best sellers. Instead, strive to build a collection that reflects the school's mission and learners. Exclusively focusing on popular titles will not push our communities to consider underrepresented voices. Curation is an opportunity for advocacy.

Carolyn's activities exemplified the School Library Alignments under the Share and Grow Domains in the Curate Shared Foundation. By including educator and learner voices, she demonstrates how "the school library facilitates the contribution and exchange of information within and among learning communities by providing an environment in which resources that support the school's curriculum and learning goals can be collaboratively selected and developed" (AASL 2018, School Library IV.C.1.). She helps her community Grow by "using local and external data to inform ongoing adjustments to the scope of the resource collection, and its audiences, formats, and applications" (AASL 2018, School Library IV.D.4.).

By looking at resources other than best sellers, Carolyn promoted "information gathering appropriate to the task by encouraging the use of information representing diverse perspectives" (AASL 2018, School Librarian IV.B.2.). Sharing diverse perspectives encourages learners to see the world through a holistic lens. When provided a variety of sources, learners can begin to systematically question and assess "the validity and accuracy of information" (AASL 2018, Learner IV.B.3.).

Weeding Collections

Weeding is complex because it is a visible activity that may be misconstrued as wasting valuable materials. Still, an important part of the Curate Shared Foundation is ensuring that the collection continues to meet the needs of the school library's users by weeding outdated or worn materials. Library director Hannah Byrd Little's thoughts address challenges that school librarians may face in weeding collections. In this example, she describes her methods for weeding to ensure a smooth process and minimize controversy.

Addressing Weeding Challenges, by Hannah Byrd Little

AVOIDING CONTROVERSY

How can we keep a fresh, clean, and up-to-date collection while keeping the controversy surrounding weeding to a minimum? I believe the key to preventing online protests and dumpster divers is transparency. I like to include other educators in the weeding process. When I have a list of aging titles, I turn them on their sides and ask specific departments to look at the volumes to see if we need to keep the books or replace them with a fresh copy. I also like to include learners when possible, even if it is just helping to move books or making sure the discarded books are donated or recycled. Sometimes we will have a used book sale. Some patrons might want an old book on flags of the world even if some of the countries in the book no longer exist.

When we ultimately do discard books, I like to use positive verbiage. Talk about freshening or growing the collection. If getting rid of the books seems painful, use Marie Kondo's advice about thanking the books before letting them go. I often talk about books going to "book heaven." I picked up this term from a college librarian when I shared a cab with her a few years ago at the ALA Annual Conference. Most of all, never think of weeding as a one-time activity. Keeping a fresh collection requires patience and is an ongoing practice.

(continued)

PRESERVING RARE BOOKS

In 1886 the Webb brothers moved The Webb School from Culleoka, Tennessee, to Bell Buckle, Tennessee. They came with $12,000 to invest in education. Of their original investment, $2,600 was spent on buildings, and $8,000 was used to purchase books. The school library was known throughout the South as having an incredible collection. More than three thousand books from this original 1880s collection were still in circulation when I joined the school in 2007. My priority was to remove all the books that were more than one hundred years old from the circulating collection. These books were not discarded; instead, they are being stored until we can assess their value. This collection move was not so controversial. However, after analysis in 2008, the average age of our overall collection was still 1976.

Because I was still new to my position, I waited until around 2010 to truly begin to weed the collection (see the accompanying table). Though we had a full collection analysis, we started merely by weeding everything over fifty years old. With these books, we set aside first editions, possible rare books, and books about local history.

Progression of the collection age at The Webb School

Year	Average Age	Books per Student
2008	1976	80
2010	1979	72
2012	1989	59
2015	1991	62
2019	1992	63

CREATING A WEEDING STRATEGY

Now in 2019, it is time to create a serious weeding strategy. Weeding such an extensive collection is a huge task. However, our school's 150th anniversary is in 2020, and we want the library to be the best it can be as we celebrate this significant event! My favorite collection analysis tool is Follett's TitleWise. You do not have to use the Follett cataloging system to analyze your collection with this tool because the TitleWise Collection Analysis supports Follett Destiny and about seven other systems. With the TitleWise system, you can view the analysis of everything from Dewey classification to reading levels.

Our weeding plan this time is not only about the age and circulation statistics of the collection but also the aesthetics. The phenomenon known as the paradox of choice was coined by psychologist Barry Schwartz, who posited that having too many choices can be overwhelming. Essentially, the idea is that we cannot see the forest for the trees or, in our case, the school library for the books.

The process of rightsizing a historic school library that is also a twenty-first-century middle and high school library will benefit from seeking some industry advice. The project will require a tremendous amount of work.

Source: Adapted from Little, 2019.

REFLECTIONS ON WEEDING COLLECTIONS

Hannah's weeding strategy considered the collection age, circulation statistics, and book aesthetics. You may not have a historic collection like Hannah's. However, *all* school libraries must be weeded regularly during the collection-development process. If you are new to your school, we recommend that you resist weeding the collection immediately. Consider these reasons for waiting:

1. Circulation statistics don't tell an entire story. New school librarians don't know what materials are used regularly yet and might weed something that educators and learners have relied on for years. Observe in-library use.
2. Weeding old books that are special to the community can damage relationships.
3. New school librarians need to understand learners and educators. Perhaps a core group of learners who love old science fiction paperbacks or educators who use the books on papermaking for a big end-of-year project will emerge.

Understanding your school's learners, educators, curriculum, traditions, and norms provides the foundation for renewing the school library through weeding. This knowledge is critical when inheriting a school library that has rarely been weeded. Again, relationships are essential.

Weeding materials directly supports School Library Alignments under the Create and Grow Domains in the Curate Shared Foundation. "The school library promotes selection of appropriate resources and tools for information use by employing a dynamic collection policy that includes selection *and retention* criteria for all materials in the collection" (AASL 2018, School Library IV.B.3., italics added). The school library also "engages the learning community in exploring resources by maintaining a collection of sufficient breadth *and currency* to be pertinent to the school's program of studies" (AASL 2018, School Library IV.D.2., italics added).

When weeding, school librarians must embrace the learner and school librarian roles to understand the changing dynamics of their collections. According to the AASL Standards, "learners select and organize information for a variety of audiences by performing ongoing analysis of and reflection on the quality, usefulness, and accuracy of curated resources" (AASL 2018, Learner IV.D.1.). Coincidently, school librarians show learners how to select and organize information by "engaging learners in ongoing analysis of and reflection on the quality, usefulness, and accuracy of curated resources" (AASL 2018, School Librarian IV.D.1.). Like Hannah, school librarians perform their analysis by engaging with their school communities to understand how a collection corresponds to the curriculum, community expectations, and needs. Hence, effective weeding requires that school librarians be simultaneously learners and educators.

Curating Experiences for Learners

Effective school librarians also curate engaging learning experiences to share with educators and learners. Elementary school librarian Kelly Hincks wrote about curating these experiences in a *Knowledge Quest* blog post. Her examples describe practices that emerged during the COVID-19 pandemic.

Like many school librarians, Kelly was adept at face-to-face teaching. But she needed to adapt to online instruction. During a discussion with her personal learning community (PLC) on Facebook, she began to consider how to develop content-driven games to play with elementary learners in a remote setting. Her research identified games that could be played in blended, face-to-face, and virtual environments.

Curating Experiences for Remote Learners, by Kelly Hincks

STAND-UP AND SIT-DOWN GAME

Stand-Up and Sit-Down is a simple movement game. All it requires is a series of questions with two options for answers, such as yes or no. Learners stand up if the answer is yes and sit down to answer no. Variations include using one or two fingers to answer or spreading arms wide for one answer and giving self-hugs for another.

SCAVENGER HUNTS

When working on a topic, have learners find something to support the lesson. For example, after reading aloud *The Legend of Rock, Paper, Scissors* by Adam Rex, learners found an object that could be used in a battle like the characters in the book. They shared the object and why it would win with their classmates as part of the discussion. Face-to-face, the game can be modified as a mental scavenger hunt where learners draw pictures of objects.

FREEZE DANCE AND LISTEN AND MOVE

After reading a book, we play Freeze Dance as an exercise to discuss the story. When the music stops, have learners answer a comprehension question. Then switch to a new dance move. For safety purposes, instruct learners to complete the activity standing in one place.

SUNKEN TREASURE GAME

Sunken Treasure is a free PowerPoint guessing game (people.uncw.edu/ertzbergerj/all-games/sunken-treasure.html) inspired through a project by Jeff Ertzberger and the University of North Carolina Wilmington. For all questions learners answer correctly, they get to select a number on the map until the hidden treasure is found. Ten different game boards featured within the PowerPoint allow gameplay multiple times with new treasure locations.

FOUR CORNERS USING JAMBOARD

Caitlyn Hanley suggested this game. Play Virtual Four Corners using Google Jamboard. Make a Jamboard and share it with learners. In each corner, numbers one through four are listed. Ask learners to write their names on a sticky note. Read a question aloud and provide four answer choices. Learners then move their sticky notes to their selected answer square.

SIXTY-SECOND SKETCH

Learners have sixty seconds to sketch something related to the topic of discussion. For example, while reading a book aloud, stop and ask learners to draw a picture of something that happened at the story's beginning.

ROLL-A-CHAT

This activity works for read-aloud discussions. Create six questions related to the book. Then roll a die and answer the question based on the number revealed. Use face-to-face with partners or as a virtual game in a group. You can also adapt the game to use Flip or Padlet for discussion. A virtual die roller can be found online.

CAPTION THIS

This game helps learners make visual connections and analyze them. It is also an excellent opportunity to show learners primary sources. The Library of Congress has several resources to explore (loc.gov/programs/teachers/getting-started-with-primary-sources). Play by showing learners a picture. Ask them to create a caption. Discuss the captions as each one is read aloud. Timers allow learners time to think. Tell learners to write their answers but wait until the timer goes off to submit them.

Source: Adapted from Hincks, 2020.

REFLECTIONS ON CURATING EXPERIENCES FOR LEARNERS

Playing games with learners may seem like a frivolous activity. If we keep in mind that our learners crave connection, camaraderie, and fun, then playing games like these can become a central element of our school library instruction. Games boost engagement. For instance, consider how scavenger hunts require learners to Think by evaluating and selecting information sources in response to an information need (AASL 2018, Learner IV.A.3.).

While fulfilling her role as a teacher, Kelly has challenged her "learners to act on an information need by designing opportunities for learners to explore possible information sources" (AASL 2018, School Librarian IV.A.2.). Kelly's creative use of gaming demonstrates how "the school library provides problem-based learning experiences and environments by using resources and technology to foster inquiry and scaffold mastery of skills necessary for learning to progress" (AASL 2018, School Library IV.A.1.). As we reflect on our curation work, let us remember that our learners, educators, and communities rely on us to curate and share more than books.

Embracing a Versatile Curation Approach

The case studies presented in this chapter demonstrate that effective Curation requires a multifaceted approach. For instance, Kimberly Johnson used a hands-on approach with a government and politics class to show how curation can be a collaborative process that evolves. In her example, the learners became curators who examined the advantages and drawbacks of creating and analyzing information sources.

Carolyn Foote's example demonstrates that curating printed materials is a process that involves seeking several information sources to construct a holistic view of available resources. Her information stream included vendors, librarians, trusted websites, journals, social media influencers, and more. Hence, curation is a discovery process that evolves with new knowledge, trends, our learners' and educators' needs, and policies that can be systematically implemented.

Hannah Byrd Little's story shows how perceptions of weeding processes are deeply interwoven into our school community cultures. It takes time to understand a collection that resides within a well-established school. The weeding process for librarians, especially those new to a school, must incorporate relationship building to be successful. Hence, weeding should not be done without acknowledging the needs, behaviors, and voices of the school community.

Finally, Kelly Hincks's creative use of games reminds us that our learners, educators, and communities rely on us to curate and share more than books. Effective school library programs connect the curriculum to curated virtual and printed resources and experiences. Experiences that support learning and enjoyment provide enriching opportunities for learners. The examples presented in this chapter provide a few ways to embrace the Curate Shared Foundation to support learning. We hope they inspire you to implement the Curate Shared Foundation's Competencies with and for your school community.

Questions for the Reflective Practitioner

1. What tips or reflections resonated with me most while reading the examples contributed by the professionals in this chapter? How did these reflections cause me to think differently about my own practice?
2. Who's a potential partner in my effort to enhance my curation? How will I involve my community as a participant in my collection-development practices?
3. How can I expand my curation practices to meet the needs of my school community and keep learners engaged?
4. What are the traditions in my school that can impact curation efforts? How will I use them to facilitate my curation efforts?

9

Understanding Curate Best Practices

At this point, you may feel various powerful, often conflicting emotions. It is natural to feel a range of emotions when considering the logistics of applying new standards to our practice. Use available resources to help you get started with the AASL Standards. In addition to the training and implementation resources provided by AASL, state chapters, blog posts, workshops, and working with our colleagues, we also have a tremendous resource under our noses. The AASL Standards are not entirely new. They reflect long-standing traditions and best practices. In this chapter, we examine and expand upon the list of Curate Best Practices found on pages 101–102 of the *National School Library Standards* book. Don't hesitate to pause and celebrate when you have already ticked one of the boxes!

Best Practices

BEST PRACTICE: Establish an advisory board of learners, parents, classroom educators, and administrators to provide input on collection-development priorities.

"School librarians work with users to select information that will be most useful" (AASL 2018, 98). One strategy for working with users is to establish a formal advisory board. Creating an advisory board will help you understand the pulse of your community. The advisory board will also serve as a sounding board for new ideas and add an element of community engagement. Moreover, "an advisory board composed of multiple stakeholder groups such as learners, parents, classroom educators, and administrators can provide input on collection priorities" (AASL 2018, 100). This element is essential for curating materials that reflect the needs of your community. If you are highly engaged with this board, there will be an added layer of protection should materials be challenged.

In addition, informal feedback will support your decision making before and after establishing a formal advisory board. Seek your community's input and feedback. "When learners and other community users share ownership of the school library and the resources available for use, the collection becomes more relevant to all users" (AASL 2018, 100). Put out a suggestion box to enable anonymous feedback. Watch the bulletin boards in the hallways for new ideas. Analyze responses to the e-mails sent out to ask for recommendations. Also, review the requests that are sent to you. Be a part of collaborative meetings with others to discuss the collection and how it can support the curriculum. In addition, create a readers' advisory group for gathering input for purchasing. Leave your desk and actively collaborate when making collection-development choices. Document *everything* that you do to embrace feedback from your community. If the school librarian is not the *only* person making collection-development choices, the school library is on its way in its Curate best practices journey.

BEST PRACTICE: Create and frequently revise a collection policy that addresses selection and retention criteria for all formats. Include a section about handling materials challenges. Be sure your administrators and school board review and sign the policy and know where it is located.

One consistency among K–12 school libraries is their inconsistency. Although many school districts and other entities have strong, frequently revised school library policies that are board-adopted and -approved, some schools and districts operate without this guidance. Wherever school librarians find themselves along this spectrum, it is advisable to seek out policies that reflect best practice and ensure that daily practice reflects the elements of sound policy, whether the governing entity formally adopts one or not.

Note that school district policies can be ambiguous and may not have been created by school librarians. If this is the case in your district, review the policy and consider how it can be improved. Then advocate for improvement. Strong collection-development policies protect the intellectual freedom of our learners and make the jobs of educators easier. As a best practice, policies should be established and followed.

Therefore, it is incumbent upon professional school librarians to continually advocate for adopting a solid collection policy with school and district leadership. When managing the library, ensure that "a collection-development policy, approved by the school board, is in place" (AASL 2018, 177). Communicate with administrators to have policies officially approved.

Start your advocacy efforts by showing how prevalent collection-development policies are among districts and by highlighting districts with suitable policies. If a library-specific policy is impossible, try connecting library collections to instructional materials policies. Many districts take this approach to justify the need for the materials.

Policies are fundamental in the school library because of the range of represented learners. School libraries serve learners with varying backgrounds and in different age groups. For example, middle school libraries have learners who have just left elementary school and others who are about to go to high school. Parents may or may not be concerned about what their students are reading. However, the presence of a policy to navigate the concerns of parents who are highly involved in their learner's education is essential for being proactive when challenges are prevalent. Specifically, stating how books are selected and the benefit of having them goes a long way to substantiate collection materials.

Finally, this is one of the most important things you should remember about the collection policy. School libraries need "an established, widely available collection-development plan, which the school librarian follows" (AASL 2018, 98). The plan must be up to date and prominently shared with your school community before there is a threat to the collection. Don't be shy about sharing the policy. The school library open house is a great time to introduce the policy. You can also include trivia questions about the policy in your newsletter. Certainly, proactivity is the key to helping our communities understand how collections are developed.

BEST PRACTICE: Frequently review the collection's contents for scope, age, and condition. Remove physical items that are out of date, infrequently used, and excessively worn. Be sure that links to digital items are still valid and that the content is still factually valid.

"Resources in the collection should frequently be reviewed for scope, age, and condition in accordance with the [collection-development] plan's provisions for weeding" (AASL 2018, 98–99). Keeping outdated materials to demonstrate a collection's extensiveness is not beneficial. Old materials, especially those related to rapidly changing subject areas such as science, can negatively impact learning. Even the parts of collections that are born digital need regular attention to verify that they are still relevant and accessible (Livanos-Propst 2019). Our learners deserve access to up-to-date materials that interest them. In addition, every school library has space limitations.

Stay on top of this task. Some school librarians choose to review collections when the library closes at the end of the year during inventory. This option is often chosen by seasoned school librarians who know their collections well. For others, however, it can be overwhelming to consider the possibility of closely examining an entire school library's physical and digital collections.

As with any enormous task, it is advisable to break it up into smaller tasks that can be accomplished over time. Set a schedule for reviewing sections of the collection, prioritizing those that get the most use. Celebrate milestones, such as when a section has been weeded, updated, refreshed, displayed, or featured. Remember to write down the part of the collection that has been reviewed. When planning your schedule, commit some time to weed. The overall idea is to review the collection frequently, which does not necessarily mean yearly, primarily if the school library is not staffed sufficiently.

Collection Evaluation Schedule Example

Consider this sample schedule for reviewing different sections of a typical school library. In the example, an attempt has been made to balance the workload, considering time constraints during shorter school months and the potential size and popularity of different sections. Another approach would be to review sections biennually, taking two months instead of one month for each designated section.

Summer: Library website and all links
September: Fiction A–E, equipment
October: Fiction F–I, nonfiction 500s
November: Fiction J–L, nonfiction 600s
December: Fiction M–N, nonfiction 900s
January: Fiction O–S, nonfiction 700s (special attention to 741.5)
February: Fiction T–W, everybody/picture/easy books
March: Fiction X–Z, graphic novels if not shelved in 741.5
April: Nonfiction 300s, nonprint, professional collection
May: Remaining nonfiction sections (000s, 100s, 200s, 400s, 800s)

Make reviewing the physical collection of books a fun event. Establish a volunteer base that can help you review books' physical condition. Pick a day to schedule a few hours for the review. Entice volunteers with recognition, snacks, and drinks. On the day of the event, put on some music. Assign each volunteer a section of shelves and ask them to scan for damaged books. Give each volunteer a clipboard and a chart to write down each damaged book's title and call number. You can review the lists later.

Avoid the misconception that you must "do it all, all at once." Rushing creates errors. Set a schedule that works for the circumstances, and change the schedule as needed. Use technology tools like Follett's TitleWise and Mackin's collection analysis tool to assist you with the task. Remember, people before things, consistently, and relax.

BEST PRACTICE: Create mechanisms for your collection's users to provide suggestions for new materials and provide feedback on existing materials.

Users who do not find themselves in a school library's collection will undoubtedly find themselves elsewhere. This statement is true at all levels but becomes even more apparent as learners enter middle and high school. Although reflected in the best practice, it bears repeating that taking steps toward making the school library for everyone through careful, collaborative curation is one of the most important aspects of ensuring the library's relevance. "Strengthen the role of the library in the community by seeking out opportunities to work with others in a mutually beneficial way, engaging stakeholders, and building relationships" (Library Leadership and Management Association [LLAMA], as cited in AASL 2018, 257).

Interest in the school library must be captured early and reinforced as learners progress to secondary education. Avoid making excuses about why learners are not visiting the school library. When you find learners not visiting the school library, invite them to special events to provide feedback. Asking learners what they want and allowing them to describe their needs strengthen curation efforts. Learners are far more attuned to diverse genres than are school librarians.

Let your learners know that their feedback is considered. When suggested titles from preferred authors arrive, feature them in displays. Post the books to the website, on social media, and in newsletters. Invite learners to provide booktalks and share them online. Moreover, create contests to inspire learners to share the resources that they have found. Ask local businesses and your parent-teacher organization to support your efforts with small prizes to increase interest.

Student library ambassadors can also identify gaps in school library collections. School librarians often rely on other educators' feedback to inform the curriculum's collection development. Learners know which assignments are challenging and whether they are finding library-curated materials. Furthermore, they can share the types of materials that they need to complete assignments. Educators may find a resource suitable, but learners note that it is too dense or dull. Speaking with educators to identify differentiated materials will ensure that the print and digital collections are being used. Suggestions mean your users are engaged, which is a win for any school library.

FIELD NOTE Supporting Classroom Educators

One purpose of the school library is to support classroom educators in their lessons. Anytime an educator thinks, "How can I best teach this?" or "What can I do about this lesson, this unit, this skill?" my job as the school librarian is to say, "I can help with that!" That might be

(continued)

in the form of resources or lessons. A big part of my job is being an authentic problem-solver alongside my teaching partners. That means I am always paying attention, listening, and trying to pick up on anything they are working through and finding a way to support those goals.

Instructionally, when I think about lessons, I think about how I can make them an authentic experience for our learners. For example, when we think about our budget and our kids' math or social studies skills, I can say, "I have *X* dollars. What do you want for the school library?" I can bring a class in and show them our makerspace catalogs, and they can propose how we should spend our budget on those makerspace materials. I did that with a third-grade class last year. It's fun for them to realize they have a voice in the school library and that their input matters. They also experience the real-life realities of limitations and working within a budget. I'm thinking about this next year for book integration. We need a pet for the school library. This activity is a fun and real problem for kids to solve. What is a good pet for our school library? It would be fun to tie this into the *Frankie Sparks and the Class Pet* book and with some of our new animal and resource books. We can tie in research skills, literature, and student voices, along with the parameters of budget and the principal's limitations.

—Heather Picciuti (elementary school librarian, Texas)

BEST PRACTICE: Ensure that your online public access catalog and collection of digital resources are available 24-7 so that users can identify and suggest needed sources, engage with digital content, and request further assistance.

The global COVID-19 pandemic demonstrated how indispensable school libraries are for face-to-face, blended, and online learning (Kapanka 2022). School librarian curation skills have been tested more intensely than at any other time in the profession's history. Providing "24-7 access ensures the greatest potential for use by most learners" (AASL 2018, 99). It can be safely said that school libraries that have successfully transitioned and have thrived as fully online information centers are far more valued and supported than those that have not.

In addition to the curation inherent in providing a robust online school library presence, we must also engage with our users online to create opportunities for them to suggest additional resources and ask us for assistance as they navigate the world of online learning. Providing opportunities does not necessarily mean that school librarians must reinvent the wheel. Embrace a PLC to assist you with learning about new trends. AASL publishes the *Knowledge Quest* journal and website. *School Library Journal* and ISTE provide similar services. State organizations offer many electronic discussion lists. ALA offers discussion boards through ALA Connect and member forums for AASL and other divisions that provide professional development throughout the year. AASL also archives town hall meetings, webinars, and other online learning in ALA's eLearning Catalog. Many of these opportunities provide complimentary access.

BEST PRACTICE: Provide classroom educators and learners with frequent updates about school library resources and their potential uses.

School librarians are expected to be leaders (AASL 2018, 14). According to LLAMA (as cited in AASL 2018, 256), "a leader effectively employs a wide range of well-developed verbal, nonverbal and written communication methods to interact." School librarians can use several modes to communicate with classroom educators and learners about resources. For example, establishing a school library website is important for timely communication. "Increased communication with stakeholders providing updates about school library resources and their potential uses to educators and learners is an additional advantage of a website of well-curated resources maintained by the school librarian" (AASL 2018, 100).

Demonstrations are also essential. It is not optimal to have an abundance of materials the community does not know how to access. Provide workshops for everyone who will listen. For example, "the school librarian frequently provides instruction in how to organize information found within resources" (AASL 2018, 97–98).

Participants may include parents, caregivers, administrators, educators, and learners. Ask your administrators for time to present during faculty meetings. Establish short morning or lunchtime presentations. Learners can be trained and recruited for outreach efforts. Other learners may find it more effective to listen to their peers. Furthermore, collect feedback on the resources that classroom educators need to learn to use. Reaching out with newsletters on platforms such as Smore can increase the school library's engagement.

FIELD NOTE Promoting the Collection with Brochures and Orientations

Promoting the school library collection is a continuous activity that provides targeted and carefully planned communication about programming and services made available to support learners', other educators', and staff members' information needs.

Library orientation is offered to educators during professional development at the beginning of the school year and again at midyear. For learners, orientation is offered around the first two weeks of the school year to introduce library services and the best approaches for accessing essential materials and relevant information. Parents and other stakeholders are presented with orientations at parent and teacher association meetings and open houses.

(continued)

> Brochures and newsletters are promotion tools created in multiple languages and digital and print formats. Creating communication using the school library website and social media platform allows for the use of audibles and videos that address patron inquiries and anticipated needs with diversity, equity, and inclusion in mind.
>
> I purposefully promote the school library collection to invite patrons to use the library and all it offers to support their academic and personal interests. Information about programming and services is available throughout the school year to highlight special events, new acquisitions, and services supporting campus literacy and learner choice.
>
> —Diane Gill (school district librarian and school librarian educator, Louisiana)

BEST PRACTICE: Create and share self-guided user supports for independent research skills and other information-seeking activities.

Teach learners using methods such as Big6 and Guided Inquiry. Invite learners with research skills to discuss how they use these processes and provide examples. "The creation of user supports that act as tutorials for independent research skills and other information-seeking activities facilitate users' seeking ways to incorporate resources collection into practice" (AASL 2018, 99). Supplement learner supports with professional development for other educators that breaks down the research process into steps. Then collaborate with classroom educators to demonstrate each step related to an assignment.

Research indicates that offering visually appealing infographics is an effective way to share print and digital resources (Parveen and Husain 2021). Creating handouts with directions for accessing digital resources and the purpose of each resource may increase usage. Embed links to video tutorials within the infographics to demonstrate how resources can be used. The school community can access these videos on demand. For example, Canva.com is available free for educators to use.

Provide opportunities for project-based learning. Remember that informal learning opportunities are also needed for learners. For instance, clubs such as filmmaking, science, creative writing, robotics, and coding encourage learners to explore practical applications of skills. The same is true of makerspaces. Inviting learners to participate in these activities allows them to practice researching areas of interest and to seek information to support independent learning. Supporting educators, learners, and families in this landscape is one of our most important activities. The practice, modeling, and instruction of the Curate Shared Foundation should take center stage.

FIELD NOTE **Creating Video Tutorials**

I create video tutorials on how to use the school's digital resources. These resources range from Google products such as Google Docs, Google Slides, and Google Forms to searching for books through the school's library management system like Follett Destiny. I embed these tutorials on my library website so learners, educators, and parents can learn how to use these tools to be successful.

—Diana Colby (high school librarian, Texas)

BEST PRACTICE: Expose learners to a variety of digital tools to describe and organize websites, digital videos, images, and other media.

Curation is about more than print materials. "Curation of resources shared through a school-based site developed and maintained by a certified school librarian ensures continuity of resources shared" (AASL 2018, 99). Learners need to know about openly available resources without the constraints of fees. Curating digital tools puts learners within reach of trending materials. It is also good practice to offer other educators frequent professional development on using digital tools.

Moreover, coordinate with school administrators to recommend and determine digital tools that will be introduced to learners and educators. Demonstrating that you are an information specialist who understands the trends will enable your school community to see you as a leader. Another effective practice is to develop how-to guides that explain the purpose of each digital tool. Model how digital tools can be crowdsourced from a PLC. Learners will be pleased to learn that gathering resources is easier than it sounds. Tools like X (formerly known as Twitter) hashtags, Google Docs, Wakelet, and Padlet allow PLCs to brainstorm and share links asynchronously. Curate lists of digital tools and periodically review the lists to determine whether the tools featured are still relevant or needed.

Digital Tools for Learners

- Apps
- Blogs
- Discussion boards and forums
- E-books
- E-mails
- Images and clip art
- MP4 files
- Podcasts
- Smartphones
- Social media
- Streaming music
- Tablets
- Video games
- Videos
- Virtual and augmented reality
- Wearable devices
- Webinars
- Wikis

BEST PRACTICE: Encourage learners to select and integrate citation recording and formatting software into their writing processes.

"School librarians work with users to select information that will be most useful, describe and organize that information, and use appropriate tools and strategies to share that information with others" (AASL 2018, 98). Teaching learners to cite information, regardless of their ages, can be difficult. Sometimes convincing educators to cite sources can be challenging. By the time learners reach college, citing sources is a critical skill to have developed. It can mean the difference between passing and failing a course. Learners must be mindful of where they get their information and how to support their statements. Teaching learners citation skills during their K–12 education sets them up for success later in life.

The beginning of the school year is a great time to teach learners how to use citation recording and formatting software. Consider visiting classrooms or inviting classes to the school library to learn about citation tools. Ask each classroom educator about the units they will complete and identify databases to assist learners with the project. Collaboratively teach about the unit and incorporate the use of citation recording and formatting software into the lessons. Tools include Mendeley, Google Scholar, EndNote Basic, Zotero, and Qiqqa. Screencast recordings with step-by-step examples of the tools in action can help remind the community how to use them.

BEST PRACTICE: Bring learners' attention to and demonstrate collection-creation and citation tools built into periodical databases.

Curation can be exhibited in many formats. "Engaging all users in the ongoing analysis of resources that best align with content curricula, personal learning needs, and interests ensures that selected information meets the requirements of the intended tasks" (AASL 2018, 98). Learning about collection creation and how to use citation tools will be more significant if learners are researching a topic that is meaningful to them. Present some real-world scenarios to learners or let them create their own. Help learners select resources that meet the needs of their chosen scenario topic. Two examples present opportunities for teaching learners to build resource lists, evaluate creditable sources, and cite resources in the collection.

Scenario One: Making a Case for Animal Shelters

A learner wants to convince their caregivers to allow them to volunteer at an animal shelter. The learner wants to understand the impact of adopted pets on families, how stray animals affect the environment, and advocacy efforts for animals. Possible resources for the learner's collection may include stories about rescued dogs, database articles about how adopted pets contribute to society, and websites about animals found in shelters. Because the learner also wants to increase the number of animals adopted, they will need resources to teach them about marketing campaigns, advertising, community outreach, and perhaps elevator speeches. Finally, ask the learner to create a presentation as a heartwarming video or in a format they choose to make a case for animal shelters. Teach the learner how to cite sources in their chosen presentation format.

Scenario Two: Starting a Business

A learner wants to start a new business and needs the support of their parents. The learner creates a list of questions to investigate, including the following:

- What supplies do you need?
- How much do supplies cost?
- How much should your product cost to earn a profit?

Resources can include ads for materials, books, and stories about youth running businesses. The learner may also wish to interview industry experts and collect journal and magazine articles related to business. Other types of information can include potential locations using Google Maps or events in town to advertise their business. The learner can locate, assess, select, and use tools to help them create flyers, banners, or a website. Their final product can be curated on a website or presentation software to support their start-up funding needs.

Thoughts on Best Practices

In all, curation is a process that changes with our communities' needs. It is important to remember that collections exist in multiple formats. Understanding how to balance these formats is a key component of providing the best access and services for the school community. As you reflect upon these best practices, decide which practice needs the most attention from you. Then implement some techniques shared in this book. Remember, your collection is only as strong as the foundation that it is built upon. Let the Curate Shared Foundation be your guide.

Questions for the Reflective Practitioner

1. Which best practice do I find the most challenging?
2. How do I plan to include my school community in implementing the best practices?
3. If I had to list my five favorite strategies for implementing the Curation best practices, what would they be? How can I get started on them today?

Conclusion: Making Connections to Curate

Curation has been a central foundation of school libraries since they were conceived. Our profession has refined the art and science of curation, as reflected in the Curate Shared Foundation, by creating policies and procedures relating to collection development. As the profession has evolved, school librarians have developed standards and professional practices put forth by AASL and other entities. These standards have provided guidelines for creating and assessing curriculums to meet the needs of the communities we serve. Providing equitable access to and instruction about carefully and thoughtfully curated resources sets the foundation for collections offered in various formats that support academic achievement, lifelong learning, and the intellectual freedom of our school communities.

School librarians have extensive experience in curating collections for learning communities, and the *National School Library Standards* present a framework for extending well-established practices in collection development beyond the traditional library collection. The AASL Standards provide the transition to using curation skills to make school libraries and programming even more central to the lives of learners, other educators, and communities. The Shared Foundations in the AASL Standards provide a comprehensive approach to using curation to facilitate inquiry, inclusion, collaboration, exploration, and engagement. Although this book has been focused on the Curate Shared Foundation, it is important to note that none of the Shared Foundations stands on its own. They are interconnected and vital to creating the school libraries and programs that our learners and educators need and deserve. Before concluding our study of Curate, we will discuss the connections between the Shared Foundations through the lens of Curate and how each is reflected in learners' behaviors.

Inquire

"The skills needed to effectively Inquire power curiosity and questioning for learners of all ages. Although individuals may not always consciously reflect on their inquiry processes, the process of asking questions, gathering information, making sense of the information, making decisions, and sharing results is something we all do every day" (AASL 2018, 28). Various motives, which may be academic, social, or perhaps born from our innate need to explain a phenomenon, can prompt us to seek answers. The question is, what do learners do with everything that they have accumulated from inquiry processes? Learners gather, organize, and put that knowledge into their mental databases to contemplate in the future. Inquiry and curation work together to ensure that when the time comes, learners can use the information they have gathered to address the disparities in their understanding of events or to help others understand the gaps in their knowledge. Hence, learners use their knowledge to build upon collective wisdom and hone their skills for the next inquiry challenge. In short, inquiry is the fuel that powers the exploration of topics and is the spark for curation behaviors.

Include

"When learners' community includes members with diverse experiences, they are aware of a range of viewpoints and anticipate the challenges often encountered in reaching consensus" (AASL 2018, 29). Considering inclusion requires the acknowledgment of diversity. Diversity allows learners to recognize, assess, and evaluate multiple viewpoints. Contributing to discussions, engaging in healthy debates, and seeking understanding by examining various perspectives are ways for learners to develop an awareness of the world. In essence, collections that reflect diversity become tools for fostering inclusive attitudes. Learners can create new knowledge by comparing and contrasting diverse perspectives with their identified resources. Once learners are confident with the content in their mental databases, they can unpack it and disseminate that content collaboratively or alone to assist with inclusive community building.

Furthermore, learners can assist others by sharing experiences or engaging in collective knowledge in safe, nurturing environments. Learners may also incorporate a new way of understanding a topic into their personal repository. Hence, learners must practice reflecting on their opinions and those of others. Reflection includes storing, unpacking, and revisiting the contents of mental databases. This process is how our learners become citizens who support equitable and inclusive practices.

Collaborate

Collaboration involves working "effectively with others to broaden perspectives and work toward common goals" (AASL 2018, 85). The curated collection that learners place in their mental databases grows continuously. Yet learners must exceed the concepts they have found alone in their journeys. Otherwise, their mental repositories will become tainted and biased from the limited perspective that informs the content. As a result, learners need to exchange with, borrow from, or work with others to fabricate new ideas. In this context, everyone becomes an educator and learner who grows their conceptual knowledge network through interactions.

Cultures are sets of assumptions, beliefs, and behaviors (Schein and Schein 2017). Learners need to examine their cultures and those around them to grow and understand the world better. Learners may find that they already know something to be true. However, when a learner cannot solve a problem alone, a new perspective can help improve their existing conceptual knowledge networks. Innovation demands the critical examination of the problem that must be solved. Seeking feedback from others about their database contents can help learners examine and revitalize their own files. Learners become empowered when they understand that change is a consistent element of life. Therefore, they must be open to collaborating to adapt previous ideas and curate new frameworks for thinking, creating, sharing, and growing.

Explore

Learners who explore "consider their existing knowledge, formulate authentic questions, experiment with physical and intellectual pursuits, collaboratively investigate answers, self-assess progress, and openly receive constructive feedback to strengthen their skills" (AASL 2018, 30). When we think of curation as building a database that holds the contents collected during an information-seeking journey, we see that curation results from exploring. Curation can be an individual or a collaborative activity to answer a question. As learners explore, they store the knowledge that they have accumulated.

Learning is a lifelong activity, and it is impossible to keep every detail. Learners must discern which materials must be eliminated to make room for new ideas. School librarians can support learners as they explore by introducing them to materials that reflect diverse viewpoints, encouraging them to investigate their interests, and teaching them how to ask questions and store new ideas in accessible formats. Embracing new ideas means that learners can examine how close they have come to the answer to a question and identify the need to seek input about the conclusions made based on the accuracy of investigative results. Moreover, pursuing new ideas leads learners to ask questions and find meaning in documents in multiple formats.

Engage

Engaged learners "demonstrate safe, legal, and ethical creating and sharing of knowledge products independently while engaging in a community of practice and an interconnected world" (AASL 2018, 113). Engaged learners are excited about their knowledge journeys and want others to know about their database contents. However, these individuals are also conscious of how to share while acknowledging the intellectual property of others and citing documents. In addition, engaged learners are aware of digital citizenship principles and use them. They know that the content they share from their database of curated materials should be vetted to ensure that any information distributed in print, verbally, or digitally is based on facts and accurately reflects the world.

Content enables learners to take part in sensemaking conversations to enrich society. Consequently, learners understand how to access knowledge to elicit meaning in future situations. Remixing knowledge permits learners to make new meanings from what is known and engage in informed decision making using documentation from various creditable sources. Curation influenced by engagement frequently results in thoughtfully disseminated knowledge reflecting balanced viewpoints.

Coming Full Circle

Ultimately, the professional role of school librarians has shifted from being the guardian of the books to being the chief information officer for school communities. Information now comes in innumerable formats, and school librarians must ensure that collections meet the needs of communities by addressing the curation of information in all forms. Curation requires a necessary shift toward technology but not necessarily away from the foundation of collecting outstanding literature, reference materials, and other informative sources contained within the books on shelves. When thinking about what it means to develop collections for users, it becomes vital that all needs are considered, not just their need for reading material.

School libraries have evolved beyond providing leisure reading, academic reading, informational text, and reference materials. School libraries have become places that empower communities to gather, explore tools, and access materials and expertise. One vital piece of knowledge that school librarians can and should provide is how to be a curator of experiences, physical and virtual spaces, tools, and collections.

As our profession moves deeper into the twenty-first century, we must teach people to overcome explicit and implicit biases. School librarians lead the way in teaching learners to find and curate the best information and resources so they can ethically and responsibly contribute to a global society. Through these curation activities, our learners will build connections between themselves and knowledge, between their knowledge and that of others, and, most importantly, between each other.

Curation Lesson Starters

Lesson starters are not complete lesson plans but provide examples of how the Curate Competencies in the *AASL Standards Framework for Learners* may be used in lesson plans. They offer a foundation on which to further develop activities for learners. Handouts can be found on learninginlibraries.com.

BOOK STUDIES WITH INTERACTIVE GOOGLE LIT TRIPS

Grade Levels: 6–9

Contributor: Amber Nabors

AASL Standards Framework for Learners:

IV.B.4. Learners gather information appropriate to the task by organizing information by priority, topic, or other systematic scheme.

Curriculum Areas: Reading, English

Activities: This lesson starter uses plot terms and Flocabulary to analyze how settings, including historical and cultural settings, influence the character and plot development. Begin by playing the Flocabulary video at flocabulary.com/unit/plot-elements. After the video, recap the plot elements of fiction that learners should be familiar with. Then, learners will read the first two chapters of *Esperanza Rising* by Pam Muñoz Ryan. While learners are reading the book, they can complete aspects of the plot mountain handout. Using Google Lit Trips, learners are expected to discuss each chapter by answering questions such as these:

- What is something you noticed?
- What is something you wonder?

Handouts and instructions for Google Lit Trips are provided at learninginlibraries.com. Learners can create an Adobe Spark Video detailing their knowledge of the beginning of the plot for *Esperanza Rising.* Consider extending the assessment to include a letter to the author explaining the importance of all parts of the plot and how that combination created a meaningful story for the learner.

Assessment: School librarians can assess learners' understanding of plot elements through their video or letter to the author.

BRINGING BOOKS TO LIFE WITH AVR (AUDIO + VISUALS + READING)

Grade Levels: 9–12

Contributor: Andy Hatcher

AASL Standards Framework for Learners:

IV.B.2. Learners gather information appropriate to the task by collecting information representing diverse perspectives.

Curriculum Areas: Reading, English

Activities: In this lesson starter, groups of two or three learners will select a diverse author to research using teachingbooks.net and answer the following question: *How do authors' life experiences impact and shape the stories they tell?*

Learners will then create an audiovisual recording of a work by their selected author to investigate the answer to the second guiding question: *How do audio-visual recordings enhance the reading experience?*

If the group chooses a children's book author, they can create a recording of the entire book for educational purposes. The recording should not be distributed or be available outside the classroom. If they choose an author who produces longer literary works, the group will produce a recording of only an excerpt.

Share with learners a basic format for the video. For instance, the biographical research about the author will introduce the video, followed by the audiovisual recording of the actual story. Each group's final product should be between five and seven minutes in duration. Learners may compile a basic video with a free program like Knovio or Microsoft Sway. Learner groups will present their recordings in class.

Assessment: The school librarian will use the presentation rubric available at learninginlibraries.com to assess the quality of the presentation content and delivery.

DIIGO: SOCIAL BOOKMARKING FOR RESEARCH

Grade Levels: 5–12

Contributor: Alissa Tudor

AASL Standards Framework for Learners:

IV.C.1. Learners exchange information resources within and beyond their learning community by accessing and evaluating collaboratively constructed information sites.

IV.C.3. Learners exchange information resources within and beyond their learning community by joining with others to compare and contrast information derived from collaboratively constructed information sites.

IV.D.2. Learners select and organize information for a variety of audiences by integrating and depicting in a conceptual knowledge network their understanding gained from resources.

Curriculum Area: Adaptable to any content area

Activities: This lesson starter focuses on the curation, evaluation, and sharing of information sites for research using diigo.com, a tool that allows users to bookmark, highlight, and tag web pages that can be retrieved from any computer. In addition, these bookmarks are collaborative and can be shared. Creating a free teacher/student account is recommended to control learner accounts and increase student privacy. You can import a CSV or e-mail invitation to add learners to a group.

Open a website and model how to highlight text on a page, add a sticky note, and find general annotation guidelines using diigo.com. This lesson activity can be adapted for any research topic. Learners will research interdependent relationships using examples from the Internet and cite their bookmarks, noting justifications. Learners will work together to bookmark websites they find during their research. Ask learners to highlight and add sticky notes/annotations while working collaboratively to create a social information library about their research topic. Learners should compile relevant web pages, videos, and pictures in addition to storing sticky notes that explain their relevance to the topic and explain the interaction. Learners should be encouraged to interact with each other's comments and expand on what their classmates have found by asking questions or commenting.

Assessment: Ideas for assessment criteria include grading for the number of stickies/annotations added to the web pages, the thoroughness of comments provided, relevant information highlighted, or the number of sources added to the school library by each user.

FORECASTING CAREERS

Grade Level: Middle school

Contributors: Diane Gill and Felecia Whitfield

AASL Standards Framework for Learners:

IV.A.1. Learners act on an information need by determining the need to gather information.

IV.B.4. Learners gather information appropriate to the task by organizing information by priority, topic, or other systematic scheme.

Curriculum Areas: Reading, Art

Activities: This lesson starter aims to guide learners in the choice of a career path using tools such as graphic organizers, a digital Wordle, and Canva.com. Tools and instructions are provided at learninginlibraries.com. This lesson is for multiple days.

Begin the lesson with a discussion about curation. Ask learners what curation means. During the lesson, model curation using various strategies and tools to organize a curated list. Provide learners examples of curation; talk about the library collection and digital resources. Consider sharing a Wakelet, Google Jamboard, or Padlet page with learners to help them understand how an individual or group of learners can curate online resources. After the discussion about curation, ask learners to complete a Frayer Model graphic organizer to summarize their understanding of curation.

Next, learners will work collaboratively in small groups to complete the K-W-L-H graphic organizer about their career interests. Ask learners again about the purpose and definition of curation. Use and generate a digital Wordle with the class based on learners' response to defining curation. Subsequently, ask learners, "What steps would you take to pursue your dream career?" Using one learner's response to the question, model how to curate a list of resources for career interests. Finally, introduce learners to Canva and teach them how to create a presentation about their dream career using the digital resources they have found.

Assessment: Learners will share their Canva presentations with classmates. Educators can also assess the completed K-W-L-H graphic organizers.

HOW TO LIBRARY: DISCOVERING SOURCES AND THE RESEARCH PROCESS

Grade Levels: 9–12

Contributor: Sierra Schuman

AASL Standards Framework for Learners:

IV.B.1. Learners gather information appropriate to the task by seeking a variety of sources.

IV.D.3. Learners select and organize information for a variety of audiences by openly communicating curation processes for others to use, interpret, and validate.

Curriculum Area: Reading

Activities: This lesson starter introduces learners to their school library's website/resources and prepares them for research. At the start of the lesson, the educator will ask several guiding questions:

- How many of you have used the school library's services before?
- How many of you have visited the school library's website before?
- What kinds of information can school libraries help students find?

Visit the school library home page and model for learners an example search related to a topic of interest. Demonstrate filters in your example search: limit results by source type, availability (physical or digital format), subject, and date published. The appropriateness of the article source selected can be evaluated by discussing authorship, description or summary, credibility, diversity, and so on. Then direct learners to conduct their own "finding" on the school library website as they practice the Think-Pair-Share technique:

Think—Learners will find specific materials from the school library catalog or database.

Pair—Working with a partner near them, learners will show what they have found and explain to their partners why they think the source is good and how they located said source (e.g., keywords used).

Share—Before the class ends, confirm whether learners found at least one source, and then ask the pairs to present what they have found together.

Assessment: Learners are assessed using a rubric provided at learninginlibraries.com that evaluates the presentation style, content, and learners' understanding of objectives.

IDENTIFYING PLAGIARISM

Grade Levels: 9–12

Contributor: Stacie Milburn

AASL Standards Framework for Learners:

IV.B.3. Learners gather information appropriate to the task by systematically questioning and assessing the validity and accuracy of information.

IV.C.2. Learners exchange information resources within and beyond their learning community by contributing to collaboratively constructed information sites by ethically using and reproducing others' work.

IV.C.3. Learners exchange information resources within and beyond their learning community by joining with others to compare and contrast information derived from collaboratively constructed information sites.

Curriculum Area: Interdisciplinary

Activities: This lesson starter introduces copyright and plagiarism concepts to learners. Important definitions and terms related to copyright and plagiarism will be discussed. Begin with the following guiding questions:

- How many of you have ever cheated on a test before?
- How many of you have copied information online, pasted it into an essay, and submitted it as your own?
- Did you know that copying another person's work and claiming it as your own is called plagiarism?

Next, introduce key terms associated with plagiarism: *copyright, intellectual property, paraphrasing,* and *verbatim.* Explain the types of plagiarism described by turnitin.com. Discuss real-world plagiarism examples, the consequences of violating copyright, and how to avoid plagiarism, and introduce important resources. A suggested presentation, handout, and whiteboard templates are provided at learninginlibraries.com. During the presentation and discussion on plagiarism, learners should use the handout to take notes on how to avoid plagiarism, important resources for understanding plagiarism, plagiarism consequences, and types of plagiarism. The "Identifying Plagiarism in the Real World" Canva whiteboard template provides videos that can be watched with learners to identify examples of plagiarism. The whiteboard activity may be extended with an opportunity for learners to collaboratively create a Google Jamboard with their responses to further the discussion.

Assessment: Read the handout responses to determine learners' understanding of plagiarism. Extend assessment by having learners react to peer reflections using emoticons on the whiteboard.

INDIGENOUS PEOPLES

Grade Levels: K–4

Contributor: Billie Corrette

AASL Standards Framework for Learners:

IV.C.3. Learners exchange information resources within and beyond their learning community by joining with others to compare and contrast information derived from collaboratively constructed information sites.

IV.D.2. Learners select and organize information for a variety of audiences by integrating and depicting in a conceptual knowledge network their understanding gained from resources.

Curriculum Areas: History, Social Studies

Activities: This lesson starter provides grade-level information and Internet research access to learners who are beginning to differentiate factual sites from non-factual sources. Begin by asking learners a guiding question—for example, "What do you know about Indigenous Peoples (Native American people)?" Learners are expected to ask questions based on what they have seen, what they have read, what they have listened to, what they have researched as a class, or any combination of these.

Activities are differentiated by grade level. Kindergarten and first-grade learners will listen to and discuss *Gluskabe Changes Maple Syrup: An Abenaki Legend*. Learners can use a storyboard to draw or write what they have learned. Second-grade learners will explore topics on PebbleGo, while third- and fourth-grade learners can be directed to sites about Native Americans, such as the Vermont Historical Society or Britannica. A supporting presentation is available at learninginlibraries.com.

Assessment: Kindergarten through first-grade learners can write or draw their answers on their storyboard maps as provided at learninginlibraries.com. Second- through fourth-grade learners will record one fact they retrieved in their search and the name of the site they used and then discuss their fact with a friend.

INFORMATION DETECTIVES

Grade Levels: 3–9

Contributor: Carmen Colon

AASL Standards Framework for Learners:

IV.A.3. Learners act on an information need by making critical choices about information sources to use.

IV.D.3. Learners select and organize information for a variety of audiences by openly communicating curation processes for others to use, interpret, and validate.

Curriculum Area: Language Arts

Activities: This lesson starter focuses on learning basic research skills while introducing web searching to young learners. Before starting the activity, ask learners questions that aim to understand their beliefs about creditable information and emphasize the need to ensure that information obtained from the Internet is reliable and accurate. Example questions may include these:

- Do you believe everything that adults tell you?
- Do you believe that what happens in movies such as the Harry Potter series is true?
- Why is it important to identify honest, accurate information?

Learners are asked to think like detectives for this activity. Show learners how to type their keywords into the search bar using the websites kidrex.org and kiddle .co. Model for learners how to document their search process using the template provided for this lesson at learninginlibraries.com. Guiding questions include the following:

- Is the site a .org, .gov, or .edu site?
- Does the site have the information I need?

If learners can answer most of the template questions, they have found a useful information resource. It is not a useful resource if they cannot answer most of the questions. After confirming that the guiding questions apply to their source, learners will apply the Detective Clues provided on the search process template to conduct their independent web searches.

Assessment: Assess learners' understanding of an Internet search through the documentation of their own search process. In addition, assess their ability to identify honest, accurate, and appropriate online sources.

INFORMATION SOURCES TREASURE HUNT

Grade Levels: 3–5
(but can be adapted for any level)

Contributors: Katie B. Loomis and Amy Lanier

AASL Standards Framework for Learners:

IV.A.2. Learners act on an information need by identifying possible sources of information.

IV.A.3. Learners act on an information need by making critical choices about information sources to use.

Curriculum Area: General (can be adapted to any subject)

Activities: This lesson starter is designed as a treasure hunt activity and will serve as a step in an inquiry-research unit designed for elementary learners. The activity will focus on using appropriate online information sources (dictionary, almanac, atlas, thesaurus, encyclopedia). Model how to navigate the school library home page using a think-aloud process to help learners find the online resources section of the home page. Click on the links for each resource and show learners how to navigate the websites to find the needed information. Learners will then complete the Information Sources Treasure Hunt worksheet provided at learninginlibraries.com by answering questions using the curated resources linked on the school library's home page. As learners complete the treasure hunt, they will signal their completion by stating, "Shiver me timbers, we found the treasure!"

Assessment: Learners will fill in the bottom section of their Treasure Hunt worksheet identifying their research topic (previously chosen) and explain their reason for choosing their information resource.

MAKING IT LEGIT: WORKS CITED PAGE MADE EASY WITH NOODLETOOLS

Grade Levels: 9–12

Contributor: Diana Colby

AASL Standards Framework for Learners:

IV.C.2. Learners exchange information resources within and beyond their learning community by contributing to collaboratively constructed information sites by ethically using and reproducing others' work.

IV.D.1. Learners select and organize information for a variety of audiences by performing ongoing analysis of and reflection on the quality, usefulness, and accuracy of curated resources.

Curriculum Areas: English I (Freshman English), Resource English I

Activities: The lesson starter's main objectives are to learn how to create a Works Cited page in NoodleTools and to create a project with citations from the Gale databases. Begin by presenting the lesson slides provided on learninginlibraries.com to the class and then assist learners in choosing topics of interest. Introduce learners to the school's Gale databases and demonstrate how to export the citations for the articles. In addition, introduce learners to Google Docs and MLA citation format. Videos are often useful in reviewing MLA guidelines and plagiarism concepts with learners. Finally, guide learners in creating a project in NoodleTools, searching for articles, using the Gale Citation Tool, and exporting to the NoodleTools project.

Assessment: Learners will be assessed on their ability to add resources to their project in NoodleTools and their ability to export a Works Cited page.

MAPPING CONNECTIONS ACROSS SOURCES

Grade Levels: 9–12

Contributor: Audrey Wilson-Youngblood

AASL Standards Framework for Learners:

IV.D.2. Learners select and organize information for a variety of audiences by integrating and depicting in a conceptual knowledge network their understanding gained from resources.

IV.D.3. Learners select and organize information for a variety of audiences by openly communicating curation processes for others to use, interpret, and validate.

Curriculum Areas: English, Social Studies, Science/STEM/STEAM

Activities: Together, learners explore a guiding question (e.g., "How can effective research techniques help me understand more about a community of interest to me?"). This lesson can be adapted for any broad topic in a subject or discipline. Learners then choose a narrower topic of interest to them to explore and curate resources. Prior to the activity in this lesson, learners will immerse themselves in exploring their chosen topic using an Internet search engine, practice evaluating online sources, and then form research questions.

Use an example research question to model and identify the keywords. Learners will then create semantic maps of keywords as they find and select resources that help them explore their questions. Show learners examples of semantic maps. Explain how researchers can map keywords to other keywords to show relationships. Demonstrate creating a list of synonyms and related terms to add to the map. Learners will apply their keywords using advanced search techniques to find and select sources in the school library's online databases. Learners will continue to add keywords to create networks of ideas across the sources they collect. Finally, learners will share their semantic maps with peers to find and form connections of ideas across their individual inquiries on the community.

Assessment: The semantic map is the assessment for this lesson. Review the content of the semantic maps and determine whether the results match the research questions for the selected topics.

MODERN-DAY WITCH HUNT

Grade Levels: 9–12

Contributor: Lacy Molina

AASL Standards Framework for Learners:

IV.C.3. Learners exchange information resources within and beyond their learning community by joining with others to compare and contrast information derived from collaboratively constructed information sites.

Curriculum Areas: Social Studies, Language Arts

Activities: In this lesson starter, learners will analyze the effects of misinformation in society by utilizing historical fiction to identify instances of misinformation in modern news stories. Learners will read *The Crucible* by Arthur Miller. Check for understanding by conducting an informal discussion to examine the story's main points. Collaborate with the classroom educator to determine the types of resources learners can use to research current events. Then review with learners the Modern-Day Witch Hunt slides and handout provided at learninginlibraries.com. Learners will work in teams or small groups to identify modern events that have escalated because of misunderstandings and compare and contrast those events with the Salem Witch Trials. The final product will be a Google document or similar product answering the questions on the Modern-Day Witch Hunt handout.

Assessment: Assess learners' ability to completely answer the questions on the handout, create references for the project, and develop a Google document (or similar end product) to share credible sources.

SHOULD ZOOS EXIST?

Grade Levels: 4–12

Contributor: Hannah Shepherd

AASL Standards Framework for Learners:

IV.B.4. Learners gather information appropriate to the task by organizing information by priority, topic, or other systematic scheme.

Curriculum Area: Reading

Activities: This lesson starter uses the OREO (Opinion, Reason, Evidence, Opinion) structure of a compelling argument to debate whether zoos should or should not exist. The starter facilitates the collection and sorting of information by learners that will become evidence for their debate and essay.

Begin by asking learners to start a K-W-L chart about zoos. Next, play these videos to build background knowledge: PBS video entitled "Are Zoos Good or Bad for

Animals?" and "Oreo Strategy Opinion Writing," a video by Detetria Funchess of Jackson Public Schools in Mississippi. After watching the videos, learners should work in pairs to complete the K-W-L chart and the lesson handout provided at learninginlibraries.com and make their cases for or against the existence of zoos. Play the PBS video a second time and prompt learners to collect evidence to substantiate their argument. The video can be watched on individual devices, and learners can pause the video to take notes about interesting facts. Circulate through the room with the classroom educator, observing learners and assisting them with taking notes and organizing their notes into categories. Finally, randomly select learners to argue for or against zoos' existence.

Assessment: Learners are assessed by the K-W-L chart completion, notes taken, and how the notes are categorized. Adapt the lesson for older learners by choosing more complex topics and including research in databases. Older learners can also be assessed by essays written to support their arguments.

TWO SIDES TO EVERY STORY

Grade Levels: 5–8

Contributor: Leila Green Little

AASL Standards Framework for Learners:

IV.B.2. Learners gather information appropriate to the task by collecting information representing diverse perspectives.

Curriculum Areas: Social Studies, U.S. History, English

Activities: This lesson starter focuses on events in American history and encourages learners to view conflicts from a dual perspective. Learners can express their opinions of the events through a written essay. To begin, ask learners to select a website recommended at weareteachers.com/history-websites. Demonstrate how to use the handout provided at learninginlibraries.com to gather information about the website they selected. The handout asks learners to identify the divergent viewpoints that caused the conflicts and how an uninvolved party could have intervened to provide a resolution. Show learners how they can use the information gathered to write an essay.

Assessment: Use the rubric provided at learninginlibraries.com to determine whether a quality essay has been written.

USING A VARIETY OF SOURCES TO CREATE INFOGRAPHICS

Grade Levels: 4–12

Contributor: Bradley Hamil

AASL Standards Framework for Learners:

IV.B.1. Learners gather information appropriate to the task by seeking a variety of sources.

IV.B.4. Learners gather information appropriate to the task by organizing information by priority, topic, or other systematic scheme.

IV.C.2. Learners exchange information resources within and beyond their learning community by contributing to collaboratively constructed information sites by ethically using and reproducing others' work.

Curriculum Areas: Reading, English, Social Studies, Science

Activities: In this lesson starter, learners choose an idea, match appropriate text evidence, and develop an infographic to provide evidence that supports the topic. Use the presentation provided at learninginlibraries.com to model an example infographic note-taker. Show learners how to fill in a source and support it with evidence. Learners should read three articles about their topic and watch one video. While learners are reading, they will collect text evidence that will be used to support their infographic and complete their graphic organizer. Check for understanding and provide feedback to each learner regarding their evidence collection. If learners are struggling with evidence collection, consider using small groups. Learners can use Piktochart and the guide in the presentation to create an infographic that supports their topic.

Assessment: The infographic with supporting evidence from at least three sources can be used as an assessment. Encourage learners to create a visually appealing infographic that includes credit for all sources.

WOMEN IN HISTORY

Grade Levels: 5–12

Contributor: Emily Novello

AASL Standards Framework for Learners:

IV.D.2. Learners select and organize information for a variety of audiences by integrating and depicting in a conceptual knowledge network their understanding gained from resources.

Curriculum Areas: Social Studies, History, English

Activities: This lesson starter engages learners in history research and an activity to connect their results to the findings of other learners. Depending on learners' grade levels, choose a strategy for introducing learners to women in history: (a) present learners with a wide variety of books, articles, and websites about women in history; or (b) teach them how to search for resources. You may also choose to assign each learner the name of a historical female figure or let learners select their own person. Then task learners with identifying an appropriate article or source about their historical figure.

Give learners a hexagonal paper shape on which they will write interesting facts about their historical figures. Subsequently, learners will collaborate by placing their hexagonal shapes side-by-side, with a volunteer placing one in the center to kick-start the process. Number each hexagonal shape. Then ask learners to make connections by relating how a fact they discovered from their reading is connected to another hexagon. Record connections on a separate handout. Challenge learners to make a connection between multiple hexagons.

The lesson can be adapted to use Google Slides instead of physical papers. Extend the lesson by placing learners in small groups of three to four members. Learners can collaborate in their small groups to determine their connections and then the groups can share their findings and make connections to other groups.

Assessment: Assess learners' ability to gather information and make connections to facts provided by others. Evaluate learners' presentation skills as they share their facts and hexagon connections.

Works Cited

AASL American Association of School Librarians. n.d.-a. "Best Digital Tools for Teaching and Learning." Accessed December 23, 2022. ala.org/aasl/awards/best.

AASL American Association of School Librarians. n.d.-b. "Common Beliefs." Accessed December 23, 2022. standards.aasl.org/beliefs.

AASL American Association of School Librarians. 2009. *Empowering Learners: Guidelines for School Library Programs.* Chicago: ALA.

AASL American Association of School Librarians. 2018. *National School Library Standards for Learners, School Librarians, and School Libraries.* Chicago: ALA Editions.

AASL American Association of School Librarians. 2019a. "National School Library Standards Crosswalk with Code with Google's CS First Curriculum." Accessed December 23, 2022. standards.aasl.org/wp-content/uploads/2019/11/aasl-standards-crosswalk-cs-first.pdf.

AASL American Association of School Librarians. 2019b. "Position Statement on Appropriate Staffing for School Libraries." Accessed December 23, 2022. ala.org/aasl/sites/ala.org.aasl/files/content/advocacy/statements/docs/AASL_Appropriate_Staffing.pdf.

AASL American Association of School Librarians. 2021. "Position Statement on the Critical Need for and Responsibilities of District-Level School Library Supervisors." Accessed June 1, 2023. ala.org/aasl/sites/ala.org.aasl/files/content/advocacy/statements/docs/AASL_School_Library_Supervisors_Position_Statement_2021.pdf.

AASL American Association of School Librarians. 2022. "Personas." Accessed December 23, 2022. standards.aasl.org/project/personas.

ALA American Library Association. n.d. "Libraries Ready to Code." Accessed December 23, 2022. ala.org/tools/readytocode/.

ALA American Library Association. 2018. "Selection and Reconsideration Policy Toolkit for Public, School, and Academic Libraries." ala.org/tools/challenge support/selectionpolicytoolkit.

ALA American Library Association Council. 2019. "Diverse Collections: An Interpretation of the Library Bill of Rights." ala.org/advocacy/intfreedom/librarybill/interpretations/diversecollections.

ALA American Library Association Council. 2022a. "Resolution to Promote Equity, Diversity, and Inclusion (EDI) Efforts in AASL While Addressing Historical Effects of Racism." Accessed December 23, 2022. ala.org/aboutala/sites/ala.org.aboutala/files/content/ALA%20CD%2052%20Resolution%20to%20Promote%20Equity_Diversity_and%20Inclusion_1.pdf.

ALA American Library Association Council. 2022b. "Resolution to Support School and Youth Services Librarians Facing Increased Intellectual Freedom Challenges." Accessed December 23, 2022. ala.org/aboutala/sites/ala.org.aboutala/files/content/ALA%20CD%2051%20Resolution%20_%20Support%20for%20School%20Librarians%20Facing%20Increased%20IF%20Challenges_1_5.pdf.

Annan, Kofi. 1997. "'If Information and Knowledge Are Central to Democracy, They Are Conditions for Development,' says Secretary-General." United Nations. Press release, June 23, 1997. Accessed May 24, 2023. press.un.org/en/1997/19970623.sgsm6268.html.

Axford, Craig. 2018. "From the Information Age to the Era of Intellectual Laziness." *Medium: The Sensible Soapbox* (blog). August 29. medium.com/the-sensible-soapbox/from-the-information-age-to-the-era-of-intellectual-laziness-104882177866.

Balzer, David. 2015. "Reading Lists, Outfits, Even Salads Are Curated—It's Absurd." *The Guardian*, April 18, 2015. theguardian.com/books/2015/apr/18/david-balzer-curation-social-media-kanye-west.

Bishop, R. S. 1990. "Windows and Mirrors: Children's Books and Parallel Cultures." Paper presented at Reading Conference, California State University, San Bernardino, March 5, 1990. files.eric.ed.gov/fulltext/ED337744.pdf#page=11.

Brown, Stacy M. 2020. *The School Librarian's Technology Playbook: Innovative Strategies to Inspire Teachers and Learners.* Santa Barbara, CA: ABC-CLIO.

Castro, Laureano, and Miguel A. Toro. 2004. "The Evolution of Culture: From Primate Social Learning to Human Culture." *Proceedings of the National Academy of Sciences* 101 (27): 10235–40.

Caulfield, Mike. 2017. *Web Literacy for Student Fact-Checkers.* pressbooks.pub/webliteracy/.

Cellucci, Anita, and Pamela Harland. 2022. "Do You Know Your Administrator's Priorities for the School Library?" *Knowledge Quest* 50 (3): 44–49.

Chant, Ian. 2020. "Mapping the Ecosystem: On Literacy, Libraries Don't Have to Go It Alone." *Library Journal* 145 (6): 34.

Chen, Diane R. 2022. "ALA Resolution 52 from AASL: Resolution to Promote Equity, Diversity, and Inclusion (EDI) Efforts in AASL While Addressing Historical Effects of Racism." March 10, 2022. Accessed June 7, 2023. tinyurl.com/365zb6ee.

Connolly, Colleen. 2022. "Anatomy of a Challenge: A Book Ban in Leander, Texas Presaged a Pattern of Challenges Nationwide." *School Library Journal* (February 1). slj.com/story/anatomy-of-a-challenge-a-book-ban-in-leander-texas-presaged-a-pattern-of-challenges-nationwide.

Creative Commons. n.d. "Six Licenses for Sharing Your Work." CC0 Public Domain Dedication. wiki.creativecommons.org/images/6/6d/6licenses-flat.pdf.

Dawkins, April M., and Emily C. Eidson. 2021. "A Content Analysis of District School Library Selection Policies in the United States." *School Library Research 24* (November). files.eric.ed.gov/fulltext/EJ1329025.pdf.

De Abreu, Belinha. 2021. "Gatekeeping Misinformation with Media Literacy Education." *Knowledge Quest* 50 (2): 26–31.

Denver Public Schools. 2016. "Academic Technology Menu." Accessed December 23, 2022. academictechnologymenu.dpsk12.org.

Donham, Jean, and Chelsea Sims. 2020. *Enhancing Teaching and Learning: A Leadership Guide for School Librarians*. 4th ed. Chicago: ALA Neal-Schuman.

Ehlers, Jillian. 2020. "The Zine Project." *Knowledge Quest* 49 (2): 34–39.

Einarsson, Árni Már, and Morten Hertzum. 2020. "How Is Learning Scaffolded in Library Makerspaces?" *International Journal of Child-Computer Interaction* 26:100199.

Foote, Carolyn. 2019. "How Do Books Get Our Attention? Library Purchasing Stories . . ." *Not So Distant Future* (blog). Accessed December 23, 2022. futura.edublogs.org/2019/01/11/what-gets-our-attention/.

Future of Privacy Forum and Software and Information Industry Association. n.d. "Student Privacy Pledge." Accessed December 23, 2022. studentprivacypledge.org/.

Google. 2023. "CS First." Accessed May 24, 2022. csfirst.withgoogle.com/s/en/home.

Graham, Rosie. 2017. "Google and Advertising: Digital Capitalism in the Context of Post-Fordism, the Reification of Language, and the Rise of Fake News." *Humanities and Social Sciences Communications* (December 12). nature.com/articles/s41599-017-0021-4.

Gross, Elizabeth A. 2022. "It Doesn't Mean What You Think It Means: Perceptions of the School Librarian and Their Work." *IASL Annual Conference Proceedings* (November 11). Accessed June 1, 2023. journals.library.ualberta.ca/slw/index.php/iasl/article/view/8554.

Hattan, Courtney, and Sarah M. Lupo. 2020. "Rethinking the Role of Knowledge in the Literacy Classroom." *Reading Research Quarterly* 55 (S1): S283–98.

Hincks, Kelly. 2020. "8 Games to Play Virtually with Elementary Students." *Knowledge Quest* (October 13). Accessed December 23, 2022. knowledgequest.aasl.org/8-games-to-play-virtually-with-elementary-students/.

Hughes-Hassell, Sandra. 2020. *Collection Management for Youth: Equity, Inclusion, and Learning*. Chicago: ALA Editions.

ISTE International Society for Technology in Education. 2023. "ISTE Standards: Educators." Accessed June 1, 2023. iste.org/standards/iste-standards-for-teachers.

Jensen, Karen. 2018. "Diversity Auditing 101: How to Evaluate Your Collection." *School Library Journal* (October 22). Accessed December 23, 2022. slj.com/?detailStory=-diversity-auditing-101-how-to-evaluate-collection.

Johnston, Melissa P. 2012. "School Librarians as Technology Integration Leaders: Enablers and Barriers to Leadership Enactment." *School Library Research* 15. ala.org/aasl/sites/ala.org.aasl/files/content/aaslpubsandjournals/slr/vol15/SLR_School_Librarians_as_Technology_Integration_Leaders_V15.pdf.

Kapanka, Heather. 2022. "School Library Media Specialists: An Evolving Profession in a Pandemic." *IFLA Journal* 48 (1): 41–49.

Katz, Stacy. 2020. "The Case for OER in LIS Education." *Library Trends* 69 (2): 419–34.

Kist, William. 2022. *Curating a Literacy Life: Student-Centered Learning with Digital Media*. New York: Teachers College Press.

Kowalski, Sue. 2022. "Joining Forces to Amplify Voice." *Knowledge Quest* 50 (5): 10–17.

Krutka, Kim R. 2022. "My Journey Toward Equity-Minded School Librarianship." *Knowledge Quest* 50 (4): 44–49.

Kuhlthau, Carol C., Leslie K. Maniotes, and Ann K. Caspari. 2015. *Guided Inquiry: Learning in the 21st Century*. 2nd ed. Santa Barbara, CA: Libraries Unlimited.

Kuykendall, Kristal. 2022. "Number of Districts Impacted by Illuminate Student Data Breach Grows as a Third Alerts Parents." *THE Journal* (April 25). thejournal.com/articles/2022/04/25/number-of-districts-impacted-by-illuminate-student-data-breach-grows-as-a-third-alerts-parents.aspx.

Lance, Keith Curry. n.d. "School Library Studies." Accessed December 21, 2022. keithcurrylance.com/school-library-impact-studies.

Lance, Keith Curry, and Debra E. Kachel. 2018. "Why School Librarians Matter: What Years of Research Tell Us." *Phi Delta Kappan* (March 26). kappanonline.org/lance-kachel-school-librarians-matter-years-research.

Lance, Keith Curry, and Leslie K. Maniotes. 2020. "Linking Librarians, Inquiry Learning, and Information Literacy." *Phi Delta Kappan* (March 26). kappanonline.org/linking-librarians-inquiry-learning-information-literacy-lance-maniotes/.

Little, Hannah Byrd. 2019. "Weeding Without Controversy: Part One—Why Weed?" *Knowledge Quest* (March 12). https://knowledgequest.aasl.org/weeding-without-controversy-part-one-why-weed.

Litvinov, Amanda. 2023. "In Appreciation of School Librarians." *NEA News* (May 17). nea.org/advocating-for-change/new-from-nea/appreciation-school-librarians.

Livanos-Propst, Athina. 2019. "Developing Weeding Protocols for Born Digital Collections." *Code4Lib Journal* 43 (February 14). journal.code4lib.org/articles/14162.

Mackey, Margaret. 2022. "Social Justice for Young Readers: Advocating for Access, Choice and Time to Read." *Literacy* 56 (2): 97–105.

Mandalios, Jane. 2013. "RADAR: An Approach for Helping Students Evaluate Internet Sources." *Journal of Information Science* 39 (4): 470–78.

Merga, Margaret K., Sayidi Mat Roni, Chin Ee Loh, and Anabela Malpique. 2021. "Revisiting Collaboration Within and Beyond the School Library: New Ways of Measuring Effectiveness." *Journal of Library Administration* 61 (3): 332–46.

Mignardi, Donna. 2021. "Graduating Information- and Media-Literate Students." *Knowledge Quest* 50 (2): 8–14.

Moeller, Robin A., and Kim E. Becnel. 2022. "School Librarians and Graphic Novel Reading: A Complicated Relationship." *The Library Quarterly* 92 (3): 259–73. doi.org/10.1086/719914.

Moreland, Denise, and Jenna Kammer. 2020. "School and Public Library Collaboration: Opportunities for Sharing and Community Connections." *Knowledge Quest* 49 (1): 41–44.

Oddone, Kay. 2021. "Storytelling with Data: Evidence-Based Advocacy." *Access* 35 (3): 10–15.

Parveen, Akthar, and Naushad Husain. 2021. "Infographics as a Promising Tool for Teaching and Learning." *Journal of Emerging Technologies and Innovative Research* 8 (8): 554–59.

Paul, Annie Murphy. 2021. "Beyond the Brain: Dynamic School Libraries Encourage Thinking with an Extended Mind." *School Library Journal* 67 (12): 67.

Philippi, Liz, and Becky Calzada. 2022. "Why Collection Development Is Important." *Knowledge Quest* 50 (4): 8–13.

Pilgrim, Jodi, Sheri Vasinda, Christie Bledsoe, and Elda Martinez. 2019. "Critical Thinking Is Critical: Octopuses, Online Sources, and Reliability Reasoning." *The Reading Teacher* 73 (1): 85–93.

Puntambekar, Sadhana. 2022. "Distributed Scaffolding: Scaffolding Students in Classroom Environments." *Educational Psychology Review* 34 (1): 451–72.

Schein, Edgar H., and Peter Schein. 2017. *Organizational Culture and Leadership.* 5th ed. Hoboken: John Wiley & Sons.

Scholastic. 2016. "School Libraries Work!" Accessed December 23, 2022. scholastic.com/SLW2016/index.html.

Schwarz, Joel. 2020. "The Cyber-Security Problem Schools and Ed. Tech Need to Face." *Education Week* (January 30). edweek.org/ew/articles/2020/01/30/the-cyber-security-problem-schools-and-ed-tech.html.

Sierpe, Eino. 2019. "Confronting Librarianship and Its Function in the Structure of White Supremacy and the Ethno State." *Journal of Radical Librarianship* 5:84–102. journal.radicallibrarianship.org/index.php/journal/article/view/39/44.

Smith, D., S. Milburn, Y. Esener, and D. Colby. 2022. "Teachers Perceptions of One-to-One Laptop Implementation: Suggestions for the Role of School Librarians." *School Library Research* 25 (May). ala.org/aasl/sites/ala.org.aasl/files/content/smith-milburn-esener-colby.pdf.

Sparks, Sarah D. 2021. "Reading on Screen vs. Print: New Analysis Thickens the Plot on Promoting Comprehension." *EdWeek* (July 22). edweek.org/teaching-learning/reading-on-screen-vs-print-new-analysis-thickens-the-plot-on-promoting-comprehension/2021/07.

Stanford History Education Group. n.d. "Teaching Lateral Reading." Civic Online Reasoning. Accessed December 24, 2022. cor.stanford.edu/curriculum/collections/teaching-lateral-reading/.

Torres, Julia, and Valerie Tagoe. 2022. *Liven Up Your Library: Design Engaging and Inclusive Programs for Tweens and Teens.* Portland, OR: International Society for Technology in Education.

Texas State Library and Archives Commission. n.d. "AASL to Texas Standards Crosswalks." Accessed December 24, 2022. tsl.texas.gov/ldn/standardssupplementalresources.

Tran, Delbert. 2016. "The Fourth Estate as the Final Check." *Case Disclosed* (blog). Yale Law School, Media Freedom and Information Access Clinic, November 22, 2016. law.yale.edu/mfia/case-disclosed/fourth-estate-final-check.

Valenza, Joyce Kasman. 2008. "Library as Domestic Metaphor." *School Library Journal Blog*. August 25. Accessed December 24, 2022. blogs.slj.com/neverendingsearch/2008/08/25/library-as-domestic-metaphor/.

Valenza, Joyce Kasman, and Wendy Steadman Stephens. 2015. "Challenging Channels: School Librarians and Evolving Literacies." *The Journal of Media Literacy* 62 (3–4): 28–38.

Van Drie, Karen, and Katie Day. 2023. "Secret International Library Networks No One Has Told You About." International Relations Round Table Webinar Series. Recorded June 8, 2023. ala.org/rt/irrt/initiatives.

Wheeler, Maurice, Debbie Johnson-Houston, and Billie E. Walker. 2004. "A Brief History of Library Service to African Americans." *American Libraries* 35 (2): 42–45. jstor.org/stable/25649066.

Whitten, C., S. Labby, and S. L. Sullivan. 2019. "The Impact of Pleasure Reading on Academic Success." *Journal of Multidisciplinary Graduate Research* 2 (1): 48–64.

Wikipedia. 2023. "Wikipedia: About." Accessed May 24, 2023. en.wikipedia.org/wiki/Wikipedia:About.

About the Authors

DANIELLA LASHAUN SMITH, PhD, MLIS, is the Hazel Harvey Peace Endowed Professor and Director of the Information Science PhD Program at the University of North Texas. She is a former classroom teacher and school and public youth services librarian. Her research has been funded by the Institute of Museum and Library Services and includes school librarian leadership, LIS education, and STEM skill acquisition in K–20 environments. The author of more than fifty publications, she has served on numerous AASL committees and has been an AASL *Knowledge Quest* blogger, chair of the AASL Educators of School Librarians Section, an ALA Councilor-at-Large, and the ALISE Director of Membership.

LEN BRYAN is the director of library services for the Houston Independent School District, where he leads the Library Services team in supporting 176 schools and almost 200,000 students. Len's previous roles include technical systems manager for Denver Public Schools; district media specialist in Hillsboro, Oregon; and school program coordinator for the Texas State Library and Archives Commission. A former middle school and high school librarian, Len served on the inaugural AASL Standards Implementation Committee from 2018 until 2020. He also serves as an advisor for Future Ready Schools.

List of Contributors

Vanessa Rivas Clouston, Round Rock Independent School District (ISD), Texas
Diana Colby, Keller ISD, Texas
Carmen Colon, Denton ISD, Texas
Billie Corrette, Barre City Schools, Vermont
Dawn Fontana, North East Independent School District, Texas
Carolyn Foote, Eanes ISD, Texas
Diane Gill, Louisiana State University, Louisiana
Bradley Hamil, Pasadena ISD, Texas
Andy Hatcher, University of North Texas, Texas
Kelly Hincks, Detroit Country Day Lower School, Michigan
Kimberly Johnson, Carroll County Public Schools, Maryland
Elizabeth Lamb, Comal ISD, Texas
Amy Lanier, Texas Woman's University, Texas
Hannah Byrd Little, The Webb School of Bell Buckle, Tennessee
Leila Green Little, University of North Texas, Texas
Katie B. Loomis, Texas Woman's University, Texas
Lesleigh Lynes, Calallen ISD, Texas
Stacie Milburn, Irving ISD, Texas
Lacy Molina, University of North Texas, Texas
Amber Nabors, Stephenville ISD, Texas
Emily Novello, Wylie ISD, Texas
Heather Picciuti, Keller ISD, Texas
Diana Rendina, Tampa Preparatory School, Florida
Trina Samson, Highline Public Schools, Washington

Sierra Schuman, University of North Texas, Texas
Hannah Shepherd, Austin Public Library, University of North Texas, Texas
Christina Stowers, Morrison Academy, Kaohsiung, Taiwan
Alissa Tudor, University of North Texas, Texas
Felecia Whitfield, DeSoto ISD, Texas
Audrey Wilson-Youngblood, Tarrant County College, Fort Worth, Texas

Index

An italicized page number indicates an illustration, table, or boxed text.